Shafted

Shafted:

The Media, the Miners' Strike & the Aftermath

SECOND EDITION

Edited by Granville Williams

CAMPAIGN FOR PRESS AND BROADCASTING FREEDOM / NORTH

Contents

*Shafted: The Media, the Miners' Strike
and the Aftermath*
Second edition
Published to mark the 35th anniversary of the miners'
strike April 2019 by the Campaign for Press and
Broadcasting Freedom (North)

Edited by Granville Williams

ISBN: 978-1-898240-10-5

Design and production: Roger Huddle

Printed by Short Run Press Limited
25 Bittern Road
Sowton Industrial Estate
Exeter

Cover: *Monday morning and shifting Everest with a
banjo* by former miner Harry Malkin. 'This painting
is really about my father. He was a ripper at Fryston
Colliery when I was growing up and when I started
there he was working his way out, as was the thing with
mining. You worked towards the face for money, then
worked out as you got older.'

Foreword
Frances O'Grady / General Secretary TUC

It's a genuine honour to introduce this second edition of Granville Williams' brilliant book *Shafted*. This updated version, featuring a wealth of new material, really enhances our collective understanding of the miners' epic struggle in 1984-85. And it exposes how powerful forces conspired against the NUM and the working-class communities it sought to defend.

The Great Strike was a defining event for working-class people and their trade unions. But it was also a human story, touching families up and down Britain, including my own. Communities suffered hardship but stood strong. Solidarity spread way beyond the pit head and built hope as well as resilience.

Inspired by the dignity of striking miners and the wonderful campaigning by Women Against Pit Closures, millions of ordinary people chose to stand with the NUM. Vilified by parts of the media, attacked by the police, targeted by a government-led class war, for a year the miners held out against all the odds. And as we knew then, the struggle was about much more than the future of coal mining – it was about the kind of country Britain was to become.

Much has changed since the first edition of the book was published, marking 25 years since the strike. Following the release of Cabinet papers, we now know the lengths to which the Thatcher government went to defeat the NUM and its members. The involvement of the intelligence services, police brutality, the collusion of shadowy business groups – every instrument of state power was deployed to crush the miners as 'the enemy within'.

Since the first edition was published, we've also seen the

establishment of the Orgreave Truth and Justice Campaign, whose events I have been proud to speak at. Given what happened at Hillsborough just a few miles away, it's high time we had a full public inquiry into government conduct and police violence at Orgreave that fateful day. *Shafted* provides further evidence why.

Above all, this book brings to life how proud working-class communities were shafted by the Thatcher government and its ruthless war on organised labour. Over three decades on, we are still living with the consequences of this unprecedented assault. With inequality rocketing and living standards stagnating, we have austerity for the many and untold riches for the few. As corporate chiefs rake it in, jobs have become more insecure, public services shredded and child poverty soars.

The campaign for justice goes on – for former pit communities and for all working people. The spirit of the miners lives on in our campaigns to end zero hours contracts, fight for decent jobs in places that need them most, defend the right to strike and organise a new generation of workers. The power lies in our own hands. If today's trades unionists show the same grit as the miners, we can not only take on the right-wing politicians, bad bosses and greedy bankers who have landed us in this mess, but this time give them the shafting they richly deserve.

Preface & Acknowledgements

This edition of *Shafted* has been produced for the 35th anniversary of the 1984-85 miners' strike. In 2009 the first edition was produced against the backcloth of the financial crash and later, after the 2010 election, the brutal austerity measures imposed by the Tory chancellor, George Osborne.

Mining communities, still reeling under the devastating impact of pit closures from 1985 through to 1994, had to suffer a second assault.

Food banks, homelessness and the hardship inflicted on people struggling with the benefits system are now widespread experiences. Ken Loach's film *I, Daniel Blake* (2016) is a powerful indictment of a faceless benefits bureaucracy that strips claimants of their humanity by reducing them to mere numbers.

Another strand of Ken Loach's film links directly back to the strike and resonates today – a celebration of the decency and kinship of ordinary people who look out for each other when the state abandons its duty of care.

It is impressive, 35 years after the miners' strike, how determined former mining communities across the UK still are to both remember the strike and to ensure that symbols of it and mining life are sustained through such diverse activities as memorials, the preservation of NUM banners or annual events like the Kent Miners' Festival and the Durham Gala.

When in 1993 Wearmouth Colliery, the last deep mine in County Durham, closed the fear was that the Miners' Gala would become irrelevant. Indeed by the mid-1990s those fears appeared to have been justified as attendances sank as low as 10,000. Instead, whilst the last coal mines closed in Nottingham and Yorkshire, we witnessed, as Huw Beynon documents in this book, a resurgence in attendance at the Gala.

Gary Cox, the chair of the Kent Miners' Festival, expresses this spirit of resistance and hope well in his contribution to *London and the 1984-5 Miners' Strike*:

We have still got solidarity. We have got people here that are still behind us and still supporting the trade unions and everything else. And I think we have achieved something. We're still fighting. Our communities are still struggling to survive.

This new edition of *Shafted* has a section dealing with the events of 1992-93 around the pit camps and protests against the Tory plans announced by Michael Heseltine in October 1992 to close 31 of the then still working 50 deep coal mines in the UK. This reflects a welcome renewed interest in that period, from Maxine Peake's play *Queens of the Coal Age* on the occupation of Parkside Colliery, to the publications *The Vigil* and *You Can't Kill the Spirit*.

I want to thank all of the people who have contributed chapters and hope they are pleased to be associated with the book. Thanks also to Roger Huddle who worked on the design and printing of the book, and to my wife Sue for proofing it. Finally, thanks for generous financial support to produce the book from the GMB (Yorkshire and North Derbyshire), NUM (Yorkshire Area), Unite (North East, Yorkshire and Humberside), and UNISON (Yorkshire and Humberside).

GW

Three Anniversaries
Granville Williams

In the calendar of struggles to uncover the truth, and battles to overturn attempts by governments to cover up injustices, 2019 is a significant year. It is the 200th anniversary of the Peterloo Massacre on 16 August 1819, when the forces of the state were deployed to squash popular protest. It is the 30th anniversary of the Hillsborough disaster on Saturday 15 April 1989, and it is the 35th anniversary of the 1984-85 miners' strike.

We hear a lot these days about 'alternative facts', 'fake news' and 'post-truth politics', but these are not new phenomena. On each of these three occasions the role of the media in establishing the 'truth' of what happened highlights that 'official' versions of events presented in the media can be deceptive, dishonest or downright mendacious.

Peterloo and Orgreave
There are many parallels between Peterloo and what happened on 18 June 1984 at Orgreave, the site of the coking plant near Rotherham, South Yorkshire:

> *The huge crowd, estimated at 60,000 people, which assembled in St Peter's Fields, Manchester, on August 16 1819 was peaceful and good humoured, and the weather was bright and sunny. But the authorities were fearful of such a display of political protest. The French Revolution was well within living memory. And after the end of the Napoleonic Wars in 1815 there had been a series of uprisings and localised violence, mainly about food and living conditions in the years of shortages and the unemployment that followed. Luddites had also broken machinery in mills across the country.*

*In Manchester, to counter these perceived threats, those
opposed to reform had created the Manchester Yeomanry in 1817, and more than 1,500 soldiers, including 340
regular cavalry from the 15th Hussars, were deployed on
that fateful day.*

Fast forward to 18 June 1984 as miners, dressed in summer attire, assembled at Orgreave, the setting for the most
violent assault by police on workers during an industrial dispute.

Thatcher's biographer Charles Moore records how she
summoned then Home Secretary Willie Whitelaw immediately on taking office in 1979 and said, "The last Conservative
government was destroyed by the miners' strike. We'll have
another and we'll win." [1] Thatcher sought to avenge the miners' victories of 1972 and 1974 and prepared meticulously
for what she saw as a crucial test of her power. In the 1980s
the police were politicised, trained in aggressive riot control
techniques and were transformed into blunt instruments to
confront workers in industrial disputes. It was in this context that the police were encouraged to dehumanise striking
miners, and the brutal assault on the miners assembled at
Orgreave by para-military police units was the consequence.

*Troops sent in to disperse the St Peter's Fields crowd
acted so aggressively that 18 people were killed and
more than 650 injured in the bloodiest political clash in
British history. In the face of these facts, the authorities
claimed the troops had been attacked first with stones
and cudgels.*

*John Tyas was The Times reporter in Manchester that
day. He had been on the platform with Orator Hunt and
was arrested. His accurate account of events appeared in
The Times on 19 August. Richard Carlile was also on the
spot to record the brutal assault by the Manchester Yeomanry and he rushed back to London to tell the story in*

W.T. Sherwin's Register where he urged Lord Sidmouth 'to bring these murderers to the bar of public justice'.

The term 'Peterloo Massacre' was coined by a local journalist, James Wroe, in punning reference to the Battle of Waterloo four years earlier. Wroe paid for this when his radical newspaper, the Manchester Observer, was closed down and he was sentenced to a year's imprisonment for seditious libel.[2]

What had happened at St Peter's Fields could not be covered up because there had been so many witnesses, but the real facts could be squashed. The government, and those sections of the press under its influence, trumpeted the conviction that the threat of revolution had been averted and moved to repress the unstamped, radical press, rushing through the Six Acts in December 1819 which extended the government's powers to control meetings, and prosecute newspapers for seditious libel.

The defeat of the miners and their return to work on 5 March 1985 had enormous repercussions, with Thatcher embarking on widespread privatisation of public utilities. She and a group of Tories around her were contemptuous of trade unions and were prepared to use the powers of the state to destroy them. The defeat of the miners enabled her to use repressive trade union legislation which allowed the government to sequestrate union funds, limit trade union solidarity and restrict the numbers of trade unionists picketing at any one time.

Lord Sidmouth, Home Secretary from 1812 to 1822, was renowned for his ruthless and efficient crackdown on dissent. He used undercover spies to gain intelligence about subversive activities and, fearful of insurrection, guaranteed that the civic authorities could rely on parliament to indemnify them if violence did break out.

Government papers released in 2014 revealed there was active "security service monitoring" of the year-long miners' strike. They reveal that surveillance was partly used to track down money belonging to the National Union of Mineworkers (NUM). The money had been hidden in bank accounts overseas to prevent its seizure by British courts. Phone tapping of NUM officials was also extensive. Seumas Milne, author of *The Enemy Within*, is clear: "Under the prime minister's guidance, MI5, police Special Branch, GCHQ and the NSA were mobilised not only to spy on the NUM on an industrial scale, but to employ agents provocateurs at the highest level of the union, dirty tricks, slush funds, false allegations, forgeries, phoney cash deposits and multiple secretly sponsored legal actions to break the defence of the mining communities."

But the full extent of this involvement is not known. Government papers dealing with security and policing were excluded from the Cabinet papers released in 2014.[3]

In the days after Peterloo, those who had orchestrated the bloody outcome celebrated. The Prince Regent sent a message recording his 'great satisfaction at their prompt, decisive and efficient measures for the preservation of the public tranquillity'. The Manchester authorities invited selected supporters to a private meeting at the police office to offer a vote of thanks to the military: 'The yeomanry had merited the entire approbation of all the respectable inhabitants of this large and populous town.'

Days after the miners' strike ended, on 27 March 1985, the government invited police chief constables to the Home Office for celebratory drinks. The reception was explained in two notes to Thatcher: 'Chief constables generally, and in particular those for Nottinghamshire and Yorkshire, made a very considerable contribution to resisting mob rule during the strike,' the first one said, 'and you might think it appropriate to say so in person.' Then, the day before the gathering, Thatcher was reminded: 'You are looking in tomorrow… for half an hour at the drinks given by the home secretary for chief constables. The idea is for you and Mr Brittan to have an opportunity to say thank you for all the police did during the miners' strike.' On the list of those attending, from 14 different forces, were Peter Wright and Tony Clement from South Yorkshire police, the force which had coordinated the assault on miners at Orgreave, fabricated evidence against miners arrested that day and charged many of them with riot.

Aftermath. Peterloo became a bitterly contested historical event. The events of that day jar with the establishment view of Britain's history, one shaped by decency, tolerance and a sense of fair play. E. P. Thompson in The Making of the English Working Class *focuses on 'the panic of class hatred' and the ingrained belief in the Manchester magistrates and the yeomanry that the working class gathering could turn into a riotous mob which justified their actions – a narrative that conveniently fits Orgreave and Hillsborough.*

Donald Read in his book *Peterloo: The Case Reopened (1958)* gives an insight into that class viewpoint. He wrote:

Peterloo is a name so well-established in English history that it is perhaps easy to forget that it is in fact a soubriquet, angrily fabricated in bitter mockery of the feat of British arms at Waterloo four years before. It first appeared in print in the Manchester Observer *newspaper on August 21, 1819. The successful designation of Peterloo as a 'massacre' represents another piece of successful propaganda. Perhaps only in peace-loving England could a death-roll of only eleven persons have been so described.*

It is a revealing comment: not enough people died to warrant the term 'massacre'.

Lesley Boulton lifts her arm as a mounted policeman attempts to club her with his baton in the iconic John Harris photo taken at Orgreave on 18 June 1984. She commented, 'The police were clearly enjoying themselves...they were excited, out of control...it felt a bit like Peterloo but without the swords.'[4]

Amber Rudd, then Home Secretary, announced her decision not to hold an inquiry into policing at Orgreave on 31 October 2016. One of the reasons she gave was there had been no deaths or wrongful convictions. Barbara Jackson, secretary of the Orgreave Truth and Justice Campaign at the time, responded, 'So it's OK that you get beaten up and seriously injured, but so long as you don't die the police don't have to be held accountable.'

The Media and the Miners' Strike

UK national newspapers are incredibly partisan and exert a powerful influence, often setting the news agenda for broadcast media. That influence is waning as the industry faces slumping ad sales, the loss of much classified advertising and precipitous drops in circulation. During the 1984-85 miners' strike it was very different.

In 1984 the average circulation of national morning newspapers was 15,487,000 and Sunday newspapers 17,827,000. A key feature of 75% of these newspapers which were owned by Rupert Murdoch (*The Sun, News of the World, The Times* and *The Sunday Times*), Fleet Holdings (*Daily Express, Daily Star* and *Sunday Express*), Associated Newspapers (*Daily Mail, Mail on Sunday*) and the The Daily Telegraph Ltd (*The Daily Telegraph, The Sunday Telegraph*) was that editorially they were strong supporters of the Conservative Party and Margaret Thatcher's brand of confrontational politics. Indeed the former Conservative MP Ian Gilmour, analysing the record of the Thatcher years, ascribes a key role to these newspapers, particular the Tory tabloids.

He observes: 'So, spurred on by a right-wing popular press which could scarcely have been more fawning if it had been state-controlled – and indeed a liberal use of the honours system to knight editors and ennoble proprietors produced much the same effect – the new Thatcher government set out to solve the problems that had defied all its predecessors since 1945.'[5]

To put it bluntly, they played a propaganda role for the government. But it was more than that. A number of editors and proprietors were powerful figures in the Conservative Party in their own right, Rupert Murdoch notably, and had got used to being deferred to. Also Thatcher was very sensitive to the inclinations of the tabloid editors, and the presentation of government policy under her was done very much in combination with them.

In addition, Peter Walker, the Energy Minister, ensured he had comprehensive information on media coverage of the strike. His Department paid £1,000 a week at one stage for a media monitoring agency to record any broadcasts on the strike. From July 1984 the presentation of both the Coal Board's and the government's case was discussed daily and he had easy access to newspaper editors and political correspondents. However Walker deliberately excluded industrial correspondents from any briefings – he regarded them as too sympathetic to the miners.

The result was that, with the partial exception of the *Mirror*, the Thatcherite mass-circulation tabloids projected a stream of front-page headlines, news reports and photographs which projected an inaccurate, partial and distorted picture of the causes and conduct of the miners' strike. These were amplified by a new development – breakfast-time television. In 1983 both the BBC *Breakfast Time* and ITV's *TV-am* started transmission. One feature on both channels was a review of the day's papers, and the tabloid front pages were given much wider coverage and impact as they were displayed prominently on these programmes.

One miner commented on media coverage: 'I object to the

way they have personalised the strike as if it's between Arthur Scargill and MacGregor because it ignores all of us on strike and our views, along with the issues we are striking for which are beginning to get lost.' Distortion and bias are created just as much by what is published or transmitted as by what isn't. Headlines supporting police and working miners dominated whilst violence inflicted on striking miners by working miners was notable by its absence.

David Thacker, a television and theatre director, commented on the interviews he tape-recorded in Barnburgh, near Doncaster, after the strike. He noted:

> Running through all the accounts we heard were two central themes. First, there was the appalling violence and brutality by the police during the strike. They were outraged no-one knew about these things. This was the second recurring theme. They were astonished by the wall of silence in the media.

If the dominant media narrative during the strike was hostile to the miners another obstacle, in terms of public opinion, was an erroneous belief that the police forces deployed against the miners were really citizens in uniform, and allegations of systematic, officially sanctioned police violence, or the use of fabricated evidence to ensure convictions, were not credible.

These issues were brought into sharp relief, and remain a topic of intense controversy, by events at the coking plant at Orgreave near Rotherham, South Yorkshire on 18 June 1984.

This much we know about Orgreave, through eyewitness accounts, film, photographs, video recordings, and the release of Cabinet papers and documents in the Thatcher Foundation: there had been picketing at Orgreave since the end of May 1984, but on 18 June the NUM mobilised 5,000 pickets from across the UK to prevent access to the works by strike-breaking lorries that collected coke for use at the British Steel Corporation mill in Scunthorpe.

The police had clearly made extensive preparations and

on that day they deployed around 6,000 officers from 18 different forces, equipped with riot gear and supported by police dogs and 42 mounted police officers. Charles Moore, the former *Daily Telegraph* editor, devotes a chapter to the 1984-85 miners' strike in the second volume of the authorised biography of Margaret Thatcher, *Everything She Wants*. 'Orgreave,' he writes, 'proved that, in enormous confrontations, the police now had the numbers, the equipment and the will to prevail.' But his account skirts over how the police prevailed.

The ITN early evening report on 18 June 1984 carried an account of the events at Orgreave which was in sharp contrast to the BBC's the same evening. The report, and the images that accompanied it, made it clear that some of the worst violence was administered by heavily-armed riot police on anyone they could catch. These actions by the police were not spontaneous, but were part of a planned operation.

The images that followed, in contrast to the BBC's, which omitted any reference to the extraordinary scenes of police violence, showed a policeman repeatedly clubbing a fallen man. An arrested man being frog-marched behind police lines yells to the ITN camera crew, 'You want to get in there and see what they are doing.' The report concluded that miners who went to help their fellow workers were being truncheoned, and the direction in which they were running demonstrated that the 'horrific violence' attributed to them was carried out in defence of fellow miners who were under attack from the police.

The BBC1's early evening news that day was completely different. Behind the newsreader, Moira Stewart, a single violent image was projected: a man taking a running kick at a policeman. The film clip of the miner attacking the police was shown again and again on BBC news programmes over the following week but it had been edited. The man was actually running back to defend one of his mates whom the police were attacking.

The scene-setting introduction for the story stated: 'Over 5,000 pickets at Orgreave fought a pitched battle with over 2,000 policemen. Mr Scargill, who had been directing operations on a two-way radio, was found sitting on a kerb looking stunned after policemen with riot shields had run by under a hail of stones. He believes he was hit by a riot shield. A senior police officer says he saw him slip off a bank and hit his head on a sleeper, but does not know whether he had already been injured.' John Thorne's report for the BBC followed, presenting three themes: the military-style planning of the operation by Arthur Scargill; doubt about whether the head injuries he sustained were actually inflicted by the police; and the essentially defensive and reactive nature of the police role in the conflict. The violence at Orgreave was presented unequivocally as picket violence, Thorne stating, 'The attacks on individual policemen were horrific. The police commanders said it was a miracle that no-one was killed.'

Of course, most of the next day's national newspapers followed the BBC version of events at Orgreave. The front page of *The Sun* had the bold banner headline 'CHARGE' with the subheading 'Mounties rout miners'. Bullet points listed 'Scargill's Toll of Shame' – 41 police injured, 82 pickets held, 28 pickets hurt – and the report by Jim Oldfield stated, 'Mounted police made an amazing cavalry charge on picketing miners yesterday. The officers faced a hate barrage of bricks, bottles and spears as they broke up a bloody riot.'

'There was a riot,' the civil liberties group Liberty observed later, 'but it was a police riot.' George Moores, the chair of South Yorkshire Police Committee at the time, said: 'No-one was stopped from going to Orgreave. They wanted to get them all together and have a real go at them... The government engineered that confrontation. The crime should be laid at their door. Their message to the police was "Go in and hit them hard." The use of dogs and horses was terrifying. They wanted Orgreave to be a media spectacle and then blame the violence on pickets.' The plan worked.

A public inquiry into policing at Orgreave would reveal much more about a number of issues that day and afterwards, in terms of policing, arrests, charges against the miners and the fabrication of evidence. But it would also have to dig into the political interventions by the Thatcher government, as well as its covert operations. This would inevitably require access to documents which are unlikely to be released for decades unless there is an independent public inquiry.

Orgreave Truth and Justice activists met the then Home Secretary, Amber Rudd, in early September 2016. Leaks from the Home Secretary's office after that meeting show a cynical process of media manipulation. She wanted to test the water before she made any decision. *The Times* published a report on 15 September citing 'Whitehall sources' saying Rudd was set to announce a limited inquiry. That unleashed a savage wave of criticism in the right-wing press (*Daily Mail*, *Daily Telegraph* and *The Times*) the following day, with Lord Tebbit, a key Cabinet member during the miners' strike wheeled out to denounce plans for an Orgreave 'show trial', while others denounced a 'costly and unnecessary official inquiry'. What was dramatically revealed was the enduring class consciousness that drove the Thatcher government in its battle with the miners. Orgreave, for those Tory diehards who had savaged Amber Rudd's possible inquiry, was the exorcism for two defeats of the previous Heath government by the miners: first at another coke depot, Saltley in East Birmingham, when 15,000 engineering workers downed tools and marched to support the miners. The Chief Constable was forced to close the gates to the depot on 10 February 1972. Then, in 1974, during another miners' strike, Heath called a general election asking the question 'who rules Britain?', and lost. So, any inquiry into Orgreave would intrude into a Tory no-go area. Amber Rudd pulled back after the vituperative media response and blocked it.

The Media and Hillsborough

It is thirty years since media coverage after the Hillsborough disaster on Saturday 15 April 1989 plumbed new depths. The focus for people's anger was, and remains, the infamous *Sun* front-page, published four days after the disaster. Even today sales of the newspaper in Liverpool are subject to a strong boycott, with even supermarkets not selling the paper.

But the media overall played a dire role in disseminating gross untruths. The disaster, unlike many others, was comprehensively recorded live in front of a TV audience and by the sports photographers there for the match. The sheer scale of the disaster attracted massive media coverage with reporters, photographers and camera crews converging on both Sheffield and Liverpool. The result was that the Sunday and Monday papers published close-up photos of Liverpool supporters either trapped, injured or dead behind the wire, graphically showing their terror and torment.

The official death list had not been published so they had no way of knowing whether the individuals pictured were alive or dead. Robert Maxwell's *The Mirror* had recently moved to full-colour and carried sixteen pages on the story, filling the front page with a grisly picture of fans who appeared dead or dying, jumbled together of top of each other, and showing blue asphyxiated bodies. I intended to buy all the newspapers that Monday to monitor coverage, but I was so appalled by *The Mirror* that I could not buy it.

What was startling about coverage in most national and regional newspapers was the certainty about who caused the disaster. The guilty charge was firmly placed on Liverpool fans. This coverage shaped public perceptions of the disaster for decades. We know now that the South Yorkshire Police (SYP) Match Commander, Chief Superintendent David Duckenfield, lied to senior officials when he stated that Liverpool fans had broken into the stadium and rushed into the central pens thus causing the fatal crush. Only when he appeared at the Warrington inquest in March 2015 did he finally admit that he had ordered gate C to be opened.

SYP disseminated a distorted, emotive and sensational version of events, and excluded any alternative explanations for the disaster. Key to this was White's News Agency, a Sheffield-based company, who circulated the SYP allegations. Their reports were based on meetings over three days between agency staff and SYP officers, interviews with Irvine Patnick MP, and the South Yorkshire Police Federation Secretary, Paul Middup. On the day of the controversial *Sun* front page, Middup told Police Federation members that 'putting our side of the story over to the press and media' had been his priority. It was a seamless narrative which fitted every prejudice about drunken Liverpool supporters, violent and ticketless, causing mayhem and death. It took the Hillsborough Independent Panel report of September 2012 to totally demolish this web of lies.[6]

The pictures and reports in newspapers triggered revulsion; the Press Council was flooded with complaints and set up an inquiry. Newspapers too were deluged with angry callers and letters. For Liverpool's bereaved families, however, the pain and anguish of such exposure was indescribable. The next wave of horror for Liverpool was the invasion of hacks charged with the grisly task of getting pictures of the dead, and tear-jerking stories from their parents, relatives and friends. Then, to add to it all, the intrusion by the media into private grief continued at funerals as the bereaved families buried their dead.

It was outrage at this state of affairs which prompted the Campaign for Press and Broadcasting Freedom (CPBF) to organise a public meeting in the iconic Bluecoats, Liverpool. The speakers were Eamon McCabe, picture editor of

The Guardian (substituting for the paper's Michael White); Steve Kelly, a former Granada producer and author of the official history of Liverpool FC, and Rogan Taylor of the Football Supporters' Association. It was a packed, emotionally-charged meeting of over 150 people struggling to cope with lies about the causes of the disaster and gross intrusions into people's grief. Steve Kelly described how his phone rang

Newspaper covers courtesy Tony Sutton collection *www.coldtype.net*

continuously: 'A week after Hillsborough I was telephoned by the producer of a leading BBC current affairs programme. "Would I like two day's work?" They wanted someone to go and knock on the doors of the bereaved and ask them if they could film the funerals and do some interviews. They had a list of a dozen names and addresses but weren't sure who had been buried. In other words I might knock on a door of a bereaved family who had already buried its dead. They did not wish to tap my knowledge of football but wanted instead to use my credibility. They knew that the reputations of journalists were at an all time low but with my association with Liverpool FC I might have been able to get access where they would be refused.'

Eamon McCabe slated the cruel and insensitive use of close-up pictures in many of the tabloids, and Rogan Taylor attacked the way the coverage of the disaster fitted into a pattern which demonised football fans, and particularly Liverpool supporters. From the audience, Brian Brierley had facts and figures relating to Hillsborough and *The Sun* newspaper and argued for a boycott of the paper in Liverpool which has been in place ever since.

The infamous *Sun* front page has become more not less toxic over the years, especially after the verdicts in Hillsborough inquests in April 2016 completely vindicated the families who had been campaigning for 27 years for the real truth, rather than the grotesque lies perpetrated by *The Sun*. The day after the *Sun* front page it carried another front page opinion piece, 'The Truth Hurts'. Well, not as much as the lies the paper relentlessly peddled under its foul-mouthed, bullying editor, Kelvin Mackenzie.

But the key issue highlighted by Hillsborough was how powerless people felt to challenge the lies being printed about Liverpool supporters and prevent the gross intrusion into people's grief. The tabloids seemed to be able to act with impunity in the absence of effective press regulation. On that front not much has changed. Then it was the Press Council, to be replaced by the Press Complaints Commission which was itself closed down. Now, in the wake of the phone hacking scandal, the Leveson Inquiry and Report, as a result of a fierce campaign by newspaper owners to resist independent regulation of the press, we have the Independent Press Standards Organisation (IPSO) set up and funded by the newspaper proprietors to regulate themselves.

Conclusion

Phil Scraton, the chair of the Hillsborough Independent Panel which produced such a powerful and devastating report in 2012, wrote: 'The documents were never lost. They lay in uncatalogued archives, unfiled cabinets and in personal collections across numerous organisations, each with institutional interests to safeguard. They were available to, but neutralised by, the process of investigation, inquiry and scrutiny. This allowed their powerful evidence to remain hidden while myth prevailed.'[7]

We should remember on the occasion of these three anniversaries how they highlight a simple truth: it is only the determination and campaigning of groups and individuals who know – in the face of official procrastination and cover-ups – that injustices have occurred, that we finally get truth and justice.

NOTES

1 Charles Moore, *Margaret Thatcher*, Vol 1, Penguin Books, 2014, p.537.

2 David Ayerst, in *Guardian: Biography of a Newspaper* (1971) has this revealing footnote on Peterloo: 'The name was a lucky invention of the extremist *Manchester Observer*.'

3 The National Archives catalogue at Kew shows that there are more than 400 files, due to have been released at the end of 2018 or before, which have been held back.

4 Michael Bailey and Julian Petley, 'The making of an icon and how the British press tried to destroy it,' in Granville Williams (ed) *Shafted: The Media, the Miners' Strike and the Aftermath*, CPBF, 2009, p92.

5 Ian Gilmour, *Dancing With Dogma*, Simon & Schuster, 1992, p2.

6 Hillsborough: The Report of the Hillsborough Independent Panel, September 2012 at: *http://hillsborough.independent.gov.uk/repository/report/HIP_report.pdf*

7 Phil Scraton,'The legacy of Hillsborough: liberating truth, challenging power,' *Race and Class*, October-December 2013, p23.

The BBC and the Miners
Tony Garnett

The bloody battle at Orgreave was not lost in the field. It was lost in the media.

Isolating the miners from other workers, indeed from the public at large, was a necessary condition of victory. Maintaining that isolation was essential to achieving it. The miners were united to the end, with the exception of Nottingham: media hostility stiffened, rather than weakened, their resolve. Thatcher could not whip them back to work, so she isolated them and waited.

The most powerful force in the world is ideology, a way of systematising knowledge that helps us to make coherent sense of our lives. Its transmitters are schools and universities. Its political power is exerted through the media. Control ideas and the people will police themselves, living within the parameters you set, unable to think outside your ideological box. It governs us largely unconsciously. Throughout the centuries the people's fight for religious, economic and political freedoms were always attempts to break free of prevailing ideologies. For almost a hundred years the BBC has been a major player in this battle for ideological power, a battle that commenced in earnest during the General Strike in 1926.

In 1925 there were 1.2 million miners. Their work fuelled the economy and helped the balance of payments. During the previous seven years pay had gone down from £6 per week to under £4.

Winston Churchill was Chancellor of the Exchequer, although he knew nothing about finance. His own finances were, as usual, in disarray. Debt pursued him all his life. The Governor of the Bank of England, Montagu Norman, together with many in the City, wanted to put the pound back on the gold standard. Churchill did so, possibly because it appealed to his love of the Imperial past.

This raised the value of the pound. Coal exports became too expensive and imports cheap enough to undercut domestic coal. Prices had to come down, so the mine owners cut wages and extended hours. The miners, who were already finding it difficult to feed their families, resisted. Their slogan was 'not a penny off the pay, not a minute on the day'.

Baldwin's Tory Government of course sided with the owners, but, just like Thatcher, he delayed the confrontation in order to prepare for the fight. The miners were supported by other workers, who knew that if the miners were defeated, they would be next, so the TUC reluctantly went along, worrying about militancy and revolutionary elements – the Bolshevik revolution was still recent memory. A General Strike loomed.

The Press Barons firmly supported the mine owners. Of course. Churchill was the editor of the Government newspaper The British Gazette. In it he wrote, 'I do not agree that the TUC have as much right as the Government to publish their side of the case and to exhort their followers to continue action.'

The miners had no voice, no way to reach the general public with their case. They were voiceless. But the Government saw a problem. The new device called the wireless was becoming popular. The manufacturers, realising that no one would buy their sets unless there was something to listen to, had created the British Broadcasting Company and appointed John Reith to run it. Churchill wanted to take it over and use it for Government propaganda.

Baldwin, a much cannier class enemy, instead did a deal with Reith. He could keep his BBC providing he toed the Government's anti-strike line. Baldwin knew that people would be more likely to believe what they heard if they thought it was independent, nothing to do with the mine owners or the Government.

Reith retained his control, thus creating the template for the mirage of independence still proclaimed by politicians. In return, throughout the strike no voice defending the miners or putting their case was heard. All the news was about strike breakers and the lack of morale among the strikers. Every voice supported the Government and the mine owners.

Reith was unperturbed. He reasoned that the elected Government was on the side of the people, he was on the side of the people, so the BBC should be on the side of the Government. His diaries reveal that he became a great admirer of Mussolini and his views were neo-Fascist.

The Labour Party, led by Ramsay MacDonald, washed its hands and walked away, as did the TUC, its leaders betraying the miners after a few days. They were left to swing in the wind and were starved back to work, on the owners' terms, many months later.

In 1984-85 the Labour leadership and the TUC again walked away, leaving the miners to fight the State in the form of Thatcher's police and biased courts. The BBC, which nearly always filmed from behind the police lines, saw the miners' self defence as the violence of the mob. You will remember the creative editing of the Orgreave footage. It opened with an image of a miner kicking a policeman. The BBC, scared of Thatcher's venom, was not about to show balance towards 'the enemy within'.

It did the BBC little good. The Director General, Alasdair Milne, was sacked by the Thatcher appointed Chairman, the right wing Marmaduke Hussey. Clearly, the BBC had to be taken even more firmly in hand.

Political obedience was not just demanded of the BBC. Thames, the ITV company, lost its franchise as punishment. Its documentary *Death on the Rock*, about the state assassination of unarmed suspected IRA members, had displeased Thatcher. It was replaced by Carlton, the shoddiest company with no history in TV. Its owner had no experience in the industry, but he was a Tory friend. He appointed David Cameron as his PR man, in his only job outside politics.

In 1965 the BBC banned Peter Wilkins' *The War Game*, a film about the consequences of nuclear war and our preparations for one. It is now generally acknowledged to be one of the most powerful films ever made in the UK. In a secret letter to the cabinet secretary, the Chairman of the Board of Governors wrote that 'showing the film on television might have a significant affect on public attitudes towards the policy of nuclear deterrence'. The ban was renewed sixteen years later, the Director General saying that he feared for the film's effect on people 'with limited mental intelligence'. By then an historical item, it was finally shown in 1985. This is a common trick. Wait until a programme has lost its power, then slide it out very late to prove how you believe in free speech.

An MI5 official had an office in Broadcasting House. He vetted applicants and refused many on political grounds. His decisions were rarely challenged by management. Even drama directors were blacklisted, although they didn't choose the subject matter or write the screenplays. They had no say over the contents. Such was the madness of it all, it was like the Stasi in East Germany.

But even more chilling were the secret reports the Security Services regularly gave to BBC News editors. They were 'background briefs' about the activities of radical and subversive political groups, tracing their involvement in strikes and campaigns. So if you thought Big Brother was watching you, you might have been correct. That was what you were paying your licence fee for.

They say the English ruling class invented hypocrisy. It is certainly very sophisticated. The BBC proclaims to the world and needs to believe of itself that it is independent of the Westminster and Whitehall establishment. Yet its very existence is predicated on funds voted by that very establishment. No wonder the BBC obeys its masters when its masters deem it necessary.

Its reputation for news was cemented during World War 2. Although the need for some official censorship in wartime was accepted by everyone, the public relied on the wireless and trusted it. During the war the BBC became the centre of national life. Its authority was respected all over the world. Its independence accepted without question. But its Chairman was a political appointment. Its supervising body, the Board of Governors, represented the great and the good. Its funds came from No 10. The Government set the licence fee.

Of course, in a two party state, there is always another party ready to take office, so both sides of the argument must be heard. This is called balance. Two politicians pretend to debate an issue under strict rules of encounter. Then they and the BBC producer go off for a drink together.

Just a few years ago both the Chairman and the Director General resigned over a brief early morning radio report suggesting the Government had lied over Iraq's possession of weapons of mass destruction. A reporter clearly didn't know how to behave. Of course, the BBC might have checked and, if the story stood up, said, 'See you in court, we stand by it.' If it did not, apologised immediately. But if you thought they might have done that, you too are under the illusion that the BBC is independent.

Never expect the BBC to see any question from the point of view of a worker, especially in the provinces. Its perspective is Westminster-based, its people live nearby and if they venture North it is as visiting anthropologists curious about the quaint customs of the natives. When do you see ordinary working people represented accurately in their dignity, as intelligent, productive adult citizens? See the world from their point of view? They are caricatured in the soaps and patronised by so-called reality TV, sensationally revealing working people as scroungers. Or thugs on strike.

On important matters the voice of the BBC is the voice of the ruling class. Any disagreements you happen to see on screen merely reveal that class in dispute with itself. During the financial meltdown after 2007, virtually all the voices interpreting the events and all the voices proposing possible solutions, were from the City or Wall Street, the very people who had caused it in the first place. No Marxist economists, scarcely even a Keynesian. No Trade Union leader. No one with a socialist perspective. The only game in town was market fundamentalism.

Why is this important?

Because one's ideological framework decides which facts are relevant and how one makes sense of them. Facts are given meaning through stories. These narratives are called The News. The people who create them think they are telling the truth, providing us with meaning so that we can better understand a complex world. They try hard to be balanced. But they work within an ideological framework the more powerful for it being unconscious. They respond to the right-wing press, which sets the daily agenda, and they must always have an eye to the wishes of their political masters.

In every newsroom stories are coming in all day. They are mostly fictions created by reporters and camera operators, offering what they think is important. Then editors choose from all this what will be included in the half hour of main news and in what order; they are all proud of having a nose for what is important. All these decisions are informed by a person's fundamental beliefs, absorbed cultural norms and 'feel' for what will be acceptable to the powers above. Is the result fact or fiction? It is certainly a point of view. How could it be otherwise? My contention that The News is the most accomplished fiction on TV was dismissed, because it is necessary for those involved in it to believe that they are dealing with facts and telling 'the truth'.

But objective truth, even in The News, is a mirage. It's an act of creation. There are many ways to attach meaning to facts. Our point of view and our unconscious bias make this unavoidable. The process begins in our families as soon as we are born: Catholic, Muslim, Man U or Arsenal. It continues in our schools. The history syllabus is the story the ruling class wants children to believe. There are many alternative histories, all hidden from children. Compare the different accounts of history taught in Britain, Germany and Russia and tell me what the truth is. If you control the narrative you control the people.

Our rulers are now panicking because they no longer control the narrative. Social media are not owned by Government: hence the complaints about 'fake news'. We are told it's the end of civilisation as we know it. The end of truth. Society will fall apart. As if our traditional media have not been throwing out fake news for generations. *The Sun*, the *Daily Mail* and other newspapers serve the agendas of their billionaire proprietors and invent facts to support their political aims. The BBC, so sanctimonious in its own defence, exists to publish the establishment line, and does so through the use of bias and exclusion. We should, indeed, be concerned about fake news. But it didn't start with the digital revolution.

Compared with most alternatives, the BBC and ITV are scrupulous in sticking to checkable facts and reporting all sides of an issue. The exceptions are areas specifically sensitive to SW1A. The BBC spends much sophisticated energy negotiating with the political establishment about what will be permitted. Tranches of senior management are occupied in this self censoring activity, much to the chagrin of its reporters.

The BBC made its reputation during World War 2. By 1945 it was secure in the hearts of the public, respected and trusted, sitting in the corner of the living room, one of the family. People had understood the need for Government censorship in the War. Despite this the BBC's brave reporters had tried to give honest witness to events, even from the front lines. From then on there was a lie at the centre of the BBC's heart, the lie that it was independent of Government, an unbiased purveyor of the truth. A detached and honest broker of facts.

Even in the face of overt Government interference, the independence of the BBC is proudly proclaimed with a straight face. To be generous, this may not be entirely hypocritical. If those administering the BBC's editorial voice are members of the same cultural and political club, often moving to Westminster from Broadcasting House and back again, graduate from the same schools and Universities, marry into each others' families and live as neighbours, they may be forgiven for not seeing the problem.

But if you are excluded from that small community there is a problem. Their news is their news, not yours. The miners in 1984-85, fighting for their jobs and their communities, discovered that they were enemies in their own country. They were treated as though they were the enemy in World War 2, traitors in fact, while the rest of the country was patriotically fighting for democracy. This was Thatcher's line so it became the BBC's line, just as it was the line of the billionaire press.

The BBC is a great national achievement. It is a publicly financed institution, seeking no private profit, its content free of commercials. That is an affront to some Tory politicians. It occupies valuable territory which would be profitable for American media corporations if vacated.That is why these Tories want to abolish it. But it is popular, even with Tory voters, so they starve it, brief against it and allow profit-making companies to make inroads into it. To soften it up. Then they hope to move in for the coup de grace. Think of the NHS as the model. They're doing the same there, under our very noses.

Because of its fine achievements we think of the BBC as family, as part of us. But it is not ours. It does not host a national conversation. In the end, when it matters, it is owned, managed and policed by those in power. It is not democratic. The people pay for it, but those who rule over us decide its policies. The country needs a BBC that belongs to the people, one genuinely independent of Government, of whatever persuasion. One whose senior management reflects the country it serves, whose editors are not just part of the Westminster bubble, but who are drawn from all social classes and experiences. A BBC whose voice is not one of privileged patronage of the provincial working class.

We must make the BBC ours if we want to achieve a real democracy.

I want a BBC that retains its historical mission to educate, inform and entertain; is free to speak truth to power; is democratised from within and without; is separated from the clutches of the Westminster conspiracy against the people; a BBC drawing together all strands of our national life and truly engaging in a national conversation.

It will be a fight to achieve it. But one worth fighting.

Taking Liberties with *Taking Liberties?*
Julian Petley

The Community Programme Unit

'Deeply biased and fundamentally damaging to BBC interests'. That was the damning verdict of George Fischer, Head Of Talks, BBC Radio, on a programme entitled *Taking Liberties?*, made with Sheffield Police Watch for the BBC Community Programme Unit (CPU) and broadcast in the *Open Space* slot on 8 November 1984. The programme showed graphic images of police violence to striking miners, and put the wind up the BBC top brass so badly that they insisted on the programme being 'balanced' by a special edition of the *Out of Court* series, which would include the President of the Association of Chief Police Officers along with a former Chief Constable and would be broadcast immediately following *Taking Liberties?*.

Before we examine what all the fuss was about, a little background information is necessary.

The BBC's Community Programme Unit was established in 1972, and the following year began producing a series called *Open Door*. The inspiration behind the Unit was the public access programming on North American cable channels. Key to its birth and development were its first Editor, Rowan Ayers, who was the former producer of *Late Night Line Up*, and the BBC's Director of Programmes, David Attenborough, to whom Ayers had pitched the idea for the Unit in the first place.

The BBC's own website describes it as 'a bold experiment in "access" TV – allowing marginalised groups to speak directly to audiences without editorial interference'.[1]

Additionally:

What made it so radical was not only that the range of

voices and opinions and styles of presentation was all suddenly and dramatically expanded; it was also that the BBC, while providing technical support and airtime, was promising to resist editorial intervention. As long as the law of the land was being observed, anything went. The draft editorial code drawn up by Attenborough stated that:

> Programme time may be offered to any group, association, organisation, community or consortium of individuals with views or activities which are not represented on the air in the course of other programming, and whose purpose is not to represent or promote a political party or group, or to pursue an industrial dispute.[2]

The code also laid down that, before being granted air time, those wanting to make programmes had to give a written undertaking that they would not use their air time, inter alia, 'as an incitement to riot or to take unlawful actions' and that they would not 'infringe the laws affecting broadcasting, e.g. defamation, contempt of court, copyright, and the Representation of the People Act'.

Open Door became *Open Space* in 1983. According to a memo from C.A. to D.G., 10 April 1984, the new series:

> …. will be filled according to the demands, needs and interests of the public. We will present programmes by, with, on behalf of those who feel themselves to be unrepresented, under-represented, or mis-represented in the mainstream of broadcasting. Above all, programmes made with the personal, social and political perspectives of those taking part.

Almost inevitably, given both series' remit, programmes caused controversy on occasion, to the very evident annoyance of the BBC hierarchy. These included programmes by an anarchist group, the English National Party, the British Campaign to Stop Immigration, the Southall Campaign Committee, and the Campaign against

Racism and Fascism. But annoyance turned to anger when programmes explicitly criticised the BBC, as did those by a Palestinian group, the Campaign for Nuclear Disarmament, the Campaign against Racism in the Media, the Campaign for Press and Broadcasting Freedom, the Glasgow University Media Group – and Sheffield Police Watch.

Taking Liberties?

Taking Liberties? had its origins in a proposal submitted to the CPU by Yvette Vanson. She had originally been offered the job of producer at the Unit in 1979, but, like many others on the Left (she was a member of the Workers' Revolutionary Party), discovered that she had been blacklisted by the BBC. She was thus prevented from taking up the post, but, thanks to the efforts of the Unit's indefatigable editor, Mike Fentiman, was offered a six months' contract as a producer in 1984.

At this point Vanson was becoming increasingly concerned at the harsh treatment by the police and the courts of the striking miners. She thus proposed a programme on the subject for *Open Space*, to be made with Sheffield Police Watch, a group of local citizens deeply concerned about the behaviour of the police and the courts, especially in Yorkshire. The proposal stated that 24 weeks into the strike 'disturbing new strategies adopted by the police have emerged which have crucial implications for the maintenance of civil liberties in Britain'. Furthermore: 'The police and the courts are usurping their traditional powers and in many cases acting beyond the law in their handling of the dispute'. For example, in the case of the police, setting up roadblocks across the country to stop the movement of pickets, abusing their powers of arrest, using excessive force, and harassing those collecting food and money for the strikers or otherwise supporting them. And in the case of the courts, attempting to criminalise secondary picketing, denying public access to specially convened 'pickets courts', imposing exceptionally stringent bail conditions, and imposing higher than average fines for the offences concerned.

A further matter for concern was the emergence of a de facto national police force, without recourse to Parliament or the local authorities, in the form of the National Reporting Centre. The proposal concludes:

> The programme would need a combination of the national (statistical) perspective – substantiated cases (stamped with the 'authority' of the solicitors and barristers) and most importantly provide a vehicle for the recounting of experiences by those directly involved (not just miners, but street collectors, villagers etc.). I also suggest an element of 'investigative journalism' – a hidden camera passing through a road block, the use of recorded incidents on the picket line and at food collections (Police Watch have audio recordings and photographs) and an attempt to show 'in actuality' these infringements of civil liberties.

The proposal was accepted, and the programme, which Vanson would produce, was put into production at short notice in August 1984 in order to fill a gap in the *Open Space* schedules which had opened up due to a planned programme dropping out. Mike Fentiman informed the Controller, BBC2, of the new programme, but unfortunately omitted to inform the Director of Programmes, Television.

Sheffield Police Watch had originally approached the CPU in June 1984. As Fentiman was belatedly to inform the Director of Programmes, Television, in a long memo dated 5 October:

> Given the 'constitutional' constraints upon the output of CPU – i.e. not to give voice to one point of view concerning current industrial dispute, the plea from Sheffield Police Watch remained at low priority for

potential selection, without our fully comprehending that their programme suggestion in no way breached the rule concerning opposing views in an industrial dispute. That is, the programme would not take sides vis-à-vis the NCB and the NUM.

However, Fentiman continued, as the dispute developed, so did the issues arising from it, and the CPU came to see that the request from Police Watch was 'proper and responsible, given the remit of the CPU', and that its members were:

.... motivated by a growing concern over the policing of the miners' dispute, with the unique perspective of being actively involved in intimately monitoring events, while remaining impartial. Their impartiality is something they repeatedly state – such impartiality, however, did not prevent them from reaching disturbing conclusions ... On the evidence Sheffield Police Watch presented to the production team, and after talking to lawyers and probation officers, it was felt that the deep concerns of the group, that civil liberties were being grossly eroded, were genuine and that a programme should be made in partnership with them.

Fentiman explained that the police were not invited, and did not ask, to appear on the programme. (It's worth noting in this respect that they were invited, but refused, to appear on the Southall Campaign Committee's controversial programme on the death of Blair Peach). He also pointed out that:

The suspicion of the mining communities of the media, for whatever reason, is well documented. Many of the witnesses necessary to support the argument that civil liberties for all are under threat as a result of the handling of this specific dispute would have, and did, refuse to appear if an opposing police view were to be given expression in the same programme. Their view was that the police have had plenty of opportunity, through the Federation, on television, in Parliament and through the Home Office to present a respectable case. This was their opportunity to present theirs.

A rebuttal exercise

The BBC hierarchy immediately showed itself to be extremely wary of the proposed programme, but allowed it to go ahead on condition that its broadcast would be immediately followed by the special *Out of Court* programme mentioned above. On 17 October, after *Taking Liberties?* had been completed, Hugh Purcell, the producer of *Out of Court*, argued in a memo to the Head of Documentary Features, Television, the editor of *Out of Court* and Mike Fentiman, that *Taking Liberties?* was 'a powerful film which we think should be broadcast' but counselled against the follow-up programme being shown immediately afterwards:

.... because the viewer will react with an expectation which cannot be met: are these allegations true or not? Have the police grossly exceeded their powers? The police, surely, will not be prepared to answer specific allegations made by the film but will react with allegations of their own re concrete blocks thrown from motorway bridges, etc. This won't get very far.

In his view, if such a programme was thought to be necessary it ought to consider the legal and policing issues raised by the strike. Legal questions would include:

How valid is the law surrounding police road blocks? ... Do the police have the right to enter homes without a warrant? Why did the miners in the police station not know they had the right to keep silent? How is the Conspiracy and Protection of Property Act being used? ... Are blanket bail conditions justified? etc.

Police questions would include:

Is there in effect a police riot squad, as alleged, and, if there is not, should there be one? Are we moving towards a national police? Is it wise to have 'foreign' police in South Yorkshire? Do the police have the right to take their numbers off their uniforms? Are the police tactics unduly militaristic?

He also suggested an introduction along the lines of:

We know there is violence on both sides, inevitably, and it is not the point of this discussion to take up the allegations or make other allegations. Instead, we are asking fundamental questions. Can the law cope with this degree of civil disorder? Can the present form of policing last for much longer? Do we need new laws, even at the risk of reducing civil liberties?

In the event, however, Purcell's suggestions were largely ignored, and the inclusion of the President of the Association of Chief Police Officers and a former Chief Constable meant that, exactly as Purcell had feared, the programme turned into a largely sterile and self-justifying rebuttal exercise by the forces of law and order. The CPU, Vanson and Sheffield Police Watch were entirely excluded from the production.

The other side

Before *Taking Liberties?* was transmitted, it was discussed at a News and Current Affairs meeting on 23 October. According to the minutes of the meeting, A.D.G (Assistant BBC Director-General, Alan Protheroe, a regular critic of the CPU) thought it had 'succeeded in communicating what it was like to be behind the picket lines, where, of course, the BBC was frequently prevented from going'. Similarly Tony Crabb argued that 'the film illustrated a serious problem which the BBC, for reasons of access, had been unable to cover as fully as it would like', whilst Alan Perry (Head of Journalism Training) 'hoped it would be explained why Sheffield Police Watch had been able to obtain the pictures while the BBC had not'.

Parrying criticism of the Corporation's coverage of the

strike by invoking problems in gaining access to the striking miners was an habitual BBC tactic. Explanations would include the general hostility/obduracy/inefficiency/of the NUM at a national level, violence or threats of violence on the picket line or at demonstrations to all representatives of 'the media', and lack of resources to cover the strike as thoroughly as the Corporation would have liked, but appears never to have been taken as an opportunity for really serious critical reflection on the BBC's coverage of the strike, or indeed of its industrial affairs coverage in general. We will return to this issue in the conclusion of this chapter.

Another feature of the BBC's dissections of the programme was the distinct impression that those concerned thought that the Corporation could have made so much better a programme on this subject if 'normal' editorial practices has been followed. Thus in the 23 October meeting:

> A.D.G. felt that such material should be shown on
> network television, but in his opinion it would have
> been better had it been incorporated in a *Panorama*
> rather than *Open Space*. But it was unlikely that
> Sheffield Police Watch, who owned the material, would
> agree to its being packaged with BBC material on the
> same subject.

Again, the reasons *why* Sheffield Police Watch might indeed be unwilling to have their material 'packaged' in line with BBC editorial principles, which would no doubt involve exactly the kind of sterile 'balancing' act attempted by tacking the *Open Court* programme onto *Taking Liberties?*, were simply left unexplored. Instead, and inevitably, the question of bias then raised its head – but not, of course, bias on the part of the BBC. So Andrew Taussig 'hoped that it would be firmly indicated that the material showed what Sheffield Police Watch claimed to be "the other side"; it should not be implied that the BBC had failed to present both sides'. Peter Ibbotson (editor, *Panorama*) wondered 'how could viewers know how genuine a picture it gave?', and George Fischer:

.... wholly agreed that the policing of the dispute should be examined. He considered, however, that it was folly to base such an examination on film that had been produced by a source about which little was known. Was the BBC not being used?

It is important to note at this point that, although most of the criticism of the programme was, and would continue to be, directed at Sheffield Police Watch, *Taking Liberties?* was made with the active involvement of the CPU, and of the programme's producer, Yvette Vanson, in particular. In an interview for the BECTU History Project, she states that:

I'd lived a bit in my life, and I liked to think I knew what was going on in the world, and I was a political woman, but I was really shocked when I went to Yorkshire and saw the extent of the police state we were living under. One of the important things about *Taking Liberties?* I think is [the sequence when] we were in a van. We tried to take a couple of miners, they were going picketing, in a van, across the border to Nottingham from Yorkshire, and we were stopped by the police and we captured it on camera. It was just absolutely devastating that we were turned back. There was no freedom of speech and there was no freedom of association.[3]

Given the previous clashes with the Unit over the programmes noted above, and also the fact that Vanson had previously been blacklisted by the BBC, it is perhaps surprising that there are few criticisms of the CPU, and none of the programme's producer, in the written records from which I have quoted in this chapter.

Issues of access and bias

The programme was broadcast on 8 November. According to the minutes of a News and Current Affairs meeting on 13 November, all of the above objections were amplified further. On the positive side, E.N.C.A.R. (John Wilson, Editor, News and Current Affairs, Radio) felt that 'the programme was justified by the points of concern which it raised and by the evidence it produced for an interpretation of events which differed from that portrayed in BBC news bulletins'. In his view, 'truth was made up of glances from different points, and the programme in question had given a viewpoint that was not normally obtained'. This is a perfectly fair point, but the reasons *why* that viewpoint was not generally available to BBC journalists were not addressed by the meeting, except by reference again to the NUM. Thus:

> Bernard Tate drew attention to the obstacles placed in the way of the BBC by the NUM, which made it impossible for the BBC itself to obtain the full picture. This was not accidental, as Peter Ibbotson pointed out, but part of the politicisation of the strike, whereby the media were lumped together with the NCB. Accepting this point, Andrew Taussig felt the result gave cause for concern; it was very worrying if relations between the BBC and a major union were so bad that it was impossible to cover a dispute such as this effectively.

Taussig also expressed the view that:

> The problem was that – rather than simply allowing minority views to be heard – programmes such as *Taking Liberties?* were dealing with mainstream topics and with material to which the BBC had been unable to gain access for practical reasons rather than because of any kind of bias.

However, it is simply impossible to separate out the issues of access and bias – in this case, BBC bias. To put it bluntly, access was difficult for many BBC journalists because, right from the start of the dispute, and based on the evidence which they saw daily on their television screens, many striking miners regarded the Corporation's national news coverage as being heavily biased against them.

Seemingly inevitably, E.N.C.A.R. asked 'how different this programme would have been if it had been under normal BBC editorial control', and expressed 'considerable reservations about the failure to label the programme as distinct from normal BBC output'. He was also uneasy about the *Radio Times* description of Sheffield Police Watch as "independent" – a term which conveyed an aura of approval. Peter Ibbotson asked 'whether the BBC had not been guilty of falling into a familiar trap; it had been so anxious to get the Police Watch material that it had been prepared to take it on any terms'. He also pointed out that the film 'might well have been pre-edited to suit the views of the group'. Hugh Purcell noted 'the one-sided approach of the programme; throughout, there had been no attempt to portray or understand police motivation', and Alan Perry expressed himself as 'reluctant to see the BBC associated with what was, in his view, blatantly biased material'. The most severe criticism came from George Fischer who saw the programme as 'deeply biased and fundamentally damaging to BBC interests':

> A conventional BBC programme would, he said, have questioned the motives of the contributors on the understanding that pictures could be used to prove anything. He felt that the BBC did itself considerable damage by suspending its normal standards of journalism to broadcast programmes of this kind.

Fischer also revealed that:

> ... his doubts extended beyond *Taking Liberties?* to the whole principle of access programming, and the convention which exempted these from normal BBC

standards and policies. He considered that a disclaimer which distanced the BBC from such programmes was merely an institutional fig leaf. The facts did not support this and, in his view, it was the editor rather than the public who set the agenda for access programmes. It was this, rather than the question of labelling, which was the real issue.

When it was pointed out that programme subjects for *Open Space* were chosen with the aid of an advisory board, Fischer questioned the extent to which the board's advice was heeded. However, Protheroe expressed 'doubts about the political complexion of the board (and hence about the advice it gave)' and 'doubts that *Open Space* was, at present, on an even keel'. He also revealed that the Director of Programmes, Television, 'was looking at the question now'. This is one of the only examples in the written record of the CPU itself coming under fire. However, this line of attack was to be vigorously pursued by the BBC hierarchy the following year, but, unfortunately, it is beyond the scope of this chapter.

Propagandist origins

Taking Liberties? was also to find itself the subject of discussion in a confidential internal BBC document, *The BBC's Journalism and the 1984/85 Miners' Strike*, written by Alan Protheroe and circulated in May 1985. Much of the comment was familiar from the News and Current affairs minutes discussed above. For example:

- 'Would it not have been preferable if the material had been shown within current affairs programmes and under the BBC's direct editorial control?'.
- 'Perhaps the greatest source of regret was that the politicisation of the strike had made it impossible for the BBC to gather the kind of material that Sheffield Police Watch had secured'.

- 'It was unfortunate that the programme had not been adequately labelled to make clear to the audience that *Taking Liberties?* should be approached in a different manner to the remainder of the BBC's output'.
- 'There were some suspicions that the group was using the BBC, and a danger that the BBC would become associated with a partisan programme that was highly critical of the police and seen by some as blatantly biased'.

This final point relates to the most serious charge levelled against *Taking Liberties?* in this document, namely that it had originated from a group 'sympathetic to the miners' point of view' and that 'the material had not been sufficiently clearly labelled so that viewers would appreciate its propagandist origins'. In these few lines are encapsulated, in unequivocal form, the BBC's fundamental objections to the programme, and, in conclusion, these need to be robustly challenged.

Unrepresented, under-represented or misrepresented

First, the purpose of the programme was not to present a point of view sympathetic to the miners. As outlined in the original proposal, and as is perfectly clear from the programme itself, its aim was to reveal highly disturbing, and quite possibly illegal, behaviour on the part of the police, and the acquiescence of the courts in this process. As stated in the original CPU editorial code quoted at the start of this chapter, the Unit would not give airtime to those whose purpose was to 'represent or promote a political party or group, or to pursue an industrial dispute'. Indeed, on 29 October 1984, a clearly beleaguered Mike Fentiman had recirculated the CPU's 'rules of application' which included 'no incitement to riot, or to violent or unlawful action of any kind' and 'no partisan presentation supporting one side only in any current industrial dispute'. He also appended the Unit's principles of selection, which included the statement:

'We make programmes with those individuals, groups, themes and issues unrepresented, under-represented or misrepresented elsewhere in the media'. *Taking Liberties?* did not infringe the rules of application and its subject matter made it a clear and obvious candidate for selection.

Second, the 'propagandist' charge – much more serious than the earlier complaints about 'bias', is wholly unsustainable, and indeed thoroughly disgraceful. The facts are these. *Taking Liberties?* showed shocking scenes of police violence and harassment and aired the testimonies of witnesses to such acts. Nothing like this had been broadcast on British television during the strike – and subsequent strike coverage would include nothing like it. Since the BBC did not want to be accused of refusing to film or broadcast such scenes, and thus of engaging in deliberate partisanship in its coverage of the strike, it had to come up with convincing explanations for their absence. As we have already seen, these included insufficient resources on the ground, and the difficulties which the BBC encountered in getting the kind of access to the picket lines which Sheffield Police Watch had done, because the pickets were hostile to 'the media'. As Protheroe put it:

> It was, of course, inevitable that much of the coverage of this dispute would be criticised irrespective of its merits. The National Union of Mineworkers, taken aback by the absence of the kind of public support that was a notable feature of the 1972 and 1974 strikes, was critical of all coverage that was not totally favourable. The hostility of much of Fleet Street towards the NUM, and in particular its leadership, led in turn to hostility on the union's part towards all sections of the media, irrespective of the nature of the coverage. This was in part designed to ensure that the NUM's case was given the fullest media coverage. An additional factor that made the volume of criticism inevitable was the divided nature of the mining

workforce, the importance of picketing in this dispute, and the television evidence of the real nature of the picketing.

However, there is actually a good deal of evidence that many of the strikers were perfectly well aware not only of the differences between the national press and the national broadcasters, but also between different sections of the broadcast media, with BBC local and regional journalists, those from *Newsnight* and individual industrial correspondents such as Nicholas Jones, along with *Channel 4 News*, being regarded as generally fair. It was journalists working for the BBC's national news programmes who were the main target of their ire – not least after the Corporation's now notorious coverage of the Battle of Orgreave.

Taken-for-granted news values and unconscious journalistic biases

Another explanation, as repeatedly noted, was to cast doubt on the *bona fides* of Sheffield Police Watch, who had, against considerable odds, managed to produce 'television evidence of the real nature of the policing', to misquote Protheroe. But why did so many senior staff at the BBC find it so difficult to believe in the veracity of the dramatic evidence which Sheffield Police Watch presented? Could it be that because such images were entirely absent from the mainstream media then there just *had* to be something suspect about them? Otherwise, why weren't they in the mainstream media? The fact that they were certainly present, and in quantity, in the radical press and in videos such as *The Miners' Campaign Tapes*, could possibly work to add further fuel to such suspicions in BBC establishment circles. In other words, the images must be the product of those with a pro-striker, anti-police axe to grind – not necessarily fabricated, but presented with a very particular slant which rendered them illegitimate in the

BBC's own journalistic terms. But such are the problems which arise when the mainstream media all follow the same agenda – anything which doesn't fit that agenda becomes 'invisible', and those who attempt to render it visible are liable to find their journalistic judgement, as well as their motives, questioned and indeed impugned. Of course, this is not to argue that the BBC was as overtly hostile to the striking miners as was the vast bulk of the national press, but nor could it be said to be impartial either – except in its own terms, which have repeatedly been shown to be highly problematic. Indeed, BBC coverage of the strike is the perfect illustration of Edward Herman and Noam Chomsky's dictum in *Manufacturing Consent* that:

> Media people, frequently operating with complete integrity and goodwill, are able to convince themselves that they choose and interpret the news 'objectively' and on the basis of professional news values. Within the limits of the filter constraints they often are objective; the constraints are so powerful, and are built into the system in such a fundamental way, that alternative bases of news choices are hardly imaginable.

Hence taken-for-granted news values and unconscious journalistic biases go unacknowledged and thus unexamined, whilst those who expose and challenge these are accused, at best, of not understanding how journalism works, or, at worst, of bias and partisanship themselves.

Battles over the Battle of Orgreave
Thus we arrive at a situation where the Assistant Director-General of the BBC, Alan Protheroe, could assert in all confidence and good faith in the above-mentioned document that, during the strike, 'the work of reporters, camera crews, producers and editors was of the highest standard and fully worthy of the BBC's traditions of fairness and objectivity' and that 'the BBC's record in reporting this

dispute is a source of considerable pride to those engaged in the Corporation's journalism', whilst, in response to similar assertions elsewhere by the Assistant Director-General, Sheffield Police Watch, in a letter to the *Guardian*, 23 February 1985, argued that they were certain that neither *Taking Liberties?* 'nor anything like it would ever have been shown under the BBC's editorial banner' and that 'in our view, based on ten months' systematic monitoring, the BBC's coverage of events on picket lines is almost as worrying as the policing we have witnessed'. Similarly *City Limits* observed at the time of the programme's broadcast that the police behaviour which it showed 'is so different from that normally seen on ITN/BBC as to reinforce every fear and suspicion about TV's pernicious role in this strike', whilst in 2016, in *History Workshop*, 82, Giles Oakley, who was a producer at the Unit at the time of *Taking Liberties?*, described it as 'one of the most important programmes CPU ever made' and 'a devastating indictment of the abuse of police power, together with damning revelations about the way the BBC had covered the strike'.

What we have here, then, are two entirely different sets of perceptions of the BBC's coverage of the strike which, in turn, are based, albeit implicitly, on radically different conceptions of what BBC journalism should be. But we cannot just leave it at that and sit on the fence: a judgement between the two has to be made. In *The BBC's Journalism and the 1984/85 Miners' Strike*, there is a section entitled 'Reflections at the End of the Strike' written by John Wilson, Editor, News and Current Affairs, Radio. In it he argues that 'it is essential that we should give people as many of the relevant facts as we can gather so that they can make moral and political judgements for themselves about the behaviour of the pickets and the behaviour of the police', and states that 'it is for our audiences to conclude whether the behaviour of the pickets is in any way qualified or justified by their case against pit closures. And whether the behaviour of the police was appropriate or excessive and intolerable'. Indeed. But if, for whatever reason, the BBC would not or could not reveal the behaviour of the police in its news and current affairs programmes that were under 'normal' editorial control, then audiences were simply not in possession of the knowledge necessary for them to make such judgements or to draw such conclusions. Thus BBC coverage of the policing of the strike has to be found seriously wanting – a judgement which is only reinforced by the vast amount of evidence of police malpractice which has come to light in subsequent years, thanks not least to the Orgreave Truth and Justice Campaign. But this is not wisdom after the event or 20:20 hindsight – the evidence was there in abundance at the time in the radical press, in the work of photographers such as Martin Jenkinson and John Harris, and in videos made by the regional film and video workshops, much of it gathered by photographers and journalists unwilling to be corralled safely behind police lines, and risking the same brutal treatment at the hands of the police as that meted out to the striking miners. Mainstream BBC news programmes chose to ignore this evidence, and, when it did manage to squeeze its way onto the BBC via the good auspices of the CPU, senior BBC staff set out to disparage and demean it. However, with very good reason, history has judged BBC national coverage of the miners' strike extremely critically, and anyone wanting to know what really happened at Orgreave on 18 June 1984 would be far better advised to watch *Taking Liberties?* (and also Yvette Vanson's subsequent *The Battle for Orgreave*, which was shown on Channel 4) than the BBC early evening news bulletin on the day of the battle itself, in which, for whatever reason, the order of the actual events of the day were reversed so that police violence against pickets was represented as a defensive action, whereas in point of fact the pickets were defending themselves against vicious attacks by the police.[4]

From Orgreave to Brexit

One would have hoped that the BBC would have learned something from the steady stream of criticism of its news coverage of the strike, and of Orgreave in particular, but the manner in which it has subsequently dealt with, for example, Brexit, the 2008 financial crisis and its aftermath, climate change and the election of Jeremy Corbyn, suggests that it has done no such thing. But, there again, the BBC is never wrong, so criticisms of its coverage are explicable to its senior staff only in terms of the biases, blinkers and bees in the bonnets of its critics.

NOTES

(1) *https://www.bbc.co.uk/historyofthebbc/people-nation-empire/opening-doors*

(2) *https://downloads.bbc.co.uk/historyofthebbc/people-nation-empire/T66-15-1%20Community%20Programmes.pdf*

(3) *www.yvettevanson.com/bectu-history-project*

(4) *www.coldtype.net/assets.16/pdf/CT128.MidNov2016.pdf*

Reflections of a return-to-work 'cheerleader'
Nicholas Jones

Once a narrative gets embedded within the popular press it can become all pervasive across the mainstream news media, and however much they might seek to uphold and defend their impartiality, broadcasters can find themselves following an agenda that might suit the government of the day. In recent years, at numerous events commemorating and debating the 1984-85 pit dispute, I have been reminded in no uncertain terms why my broadcasts were so resented in the final months of the strike: my voice was regarded as that of a cheerleader for the return to work. NUM activists have told me how, when having breakfast on Monday mornings before starting another week on picket-line duty, they would hear my early morning reports for BBC radio giving the latest figures for the number of 'new faces', as they were known, returning to work.

When half the miners were back Margaret Thatcher intended to claim victory, which is precisely what she did, and the 'new faces' were the heroes of the tabloid press. As the momentum built up behind the push to accelerate the return to work, the total number of men said to be giving up the strike each week became headline news. Inevitably these reports tended to be one sided: I was having to rely, as were other newsrooms, on information collated from colliery managers around the coalfields, backed up wherever possible by eye-witness reports from journalists at pit gates. There was a dearth of up-to-date statistical information from the NUM. Other than issuing a blanket denial of the figures which journalists were quoting, which was hardly surprising given the determination to sustain the strikers' solidarity, the union refused to play what the NUM President, Arthur

Scargill, dismissed as the news media's numbers game.

Just like the sustained scare story over the existence of weapons of mass destruction which preceded the 2003 Iraq War, the year-long pit dispute was played out against an equally well-entrenched narrative aimed at demonising the miners as the 'enemy within'. For the British news media, the confrontation between Thatcher and Scargill had as much potency as the subsequent fight to the finish to defeat the Iraqi President, Saddam Hussein. Many journalists have reflected ruefully on the way they were taken in by the pro-war propaganda of George Bush and Tony Blair in the months leading up to the American-led invasion in March 2003. Similarly, when I think back to my reporting of the 1984-85 miners' strike, I have to admit that in the end I found myself ensnared by the seeming inevitability of the Thatcherite storyline that the mineworkers had to be defeated in order to smash trade union militancy.

In the years that have elapsed I have been forced to explain the inherent dangers in being caught up in the type of agenda-setting that the combined forces of the state are only too happy to manipulate. One of the many pointed reminders of the need for some soul-searching on my part followed a television interview for the 20th anniversary of the strike by Thatcher's favourite propagandist, Tim Bell, who was chief media adviser during the strike to the chairman of the National Coal Board, Ian MacGregor. Bell put into stark perspective the sense of despair that those pickets must have experienced on hearing my Monday morning reports. He outlined the media strategy of the Prime Minister's advisers: "We wanted the strikers to drag themselves back to work, their tails between their legs. That was what it was all about at the end."

With the benefit of hindsight, and the subsequent evidence of a vindictive pit closure programme that continued during the decade which followed the strike, perhaps the news media should own up to a collective failure of judgement comparable to that during the build-up to the Iraq War. As most journalists have since acknowledged, not enough was done to question the accuracy of the pre-war intelligence reports, so as to determine the true nature of the threat posed by Iraq's chemical and biological weapons. Likewise, the same charge could perhaps be levelled against the industrial and labour correspondents of the 1980s.

My erstwhile colleagues might not agree with my conclusion, but I don't think any of us ever imagined that such was the Conservative Party's contempt for the NCB, and so great was the Thatcherite fear and hatred of the NUM, that the Tories would end up all but destroying the British coal industry and marginalising a valuable source of energy. Perhaps we should have been much more sceptical and far smarter in challenging the true intentions of ministers and the coal board management. For my own part, I probably took it for granted that the Conservatives still believed that coal had a future once the uneconomic pits had been closed. I certainly did not suspect that the Tories would force through a closure programme that would exceed even the direst predictions of the NUM President and his claims about the existence of a hidden 'hit list' of pits to be closed.

To Scargill and many union activists the dividing line could not have been clearer: journalists were part and parcel of the class enemy and he always predicted they would instinctively support Thatcher. That charge was reinforced in April 2004 during events to mark the 20th anniversary of the strike when, in his role as the union's honorary president, Scargill accused the news media of seeking to rewrite events by trying to deny that their endurance had made it 'the most principled struggle in British trade union history'.

While I would contend that broadcasters like myself tried valiantly to present both sides of the dispute, we did have to work within what had become an all-embracing, all-powerful narrative: the country could not afford to continue subsidising uneconomic coal mines, devastating though that might be for their communities; the strike itself was a denial of democracy because there had been no pit head ballot; and the violence on the miners' picket lines, by challenging the rule of law, constituted a threat to the democratic government of the country.

In the final months of the strike, once it became clear there was no longer any chance of a negotiated settlement, the balance of coverage tipped almost completely in the management's favour. I do accept, as argued subsequently by the Campaign for Press and Broadcasting Freedom in its 1985 publication, *Media Hits The Pits*, that most radio and television journalists became, in effect, the cheerleaders for the return to work. By the later stages of the dispute, the narrative had been condensed into a simpler, far clearer story line: the outcome would depend on the NCB's success in persuading miners to abandon the strike and return to their pits.

Spending a full year concentrating almost exclusively on reporting just one dispute was for me a new and unique experience. Thatcher was at the height of her power and, except for titles such as the *Daily Mirror, The Guardian* and *Morning Star*, she had the overwhelming support of the national press. Most tabloids were in full propaganda mode, backing the Prime Minister every step of the way while condemning what they argued was the illegality of the strike, the lawlessness and violence of the pickets, and Scargill's obdurate refusal to accept the closure of any loss-making pits. Providing press encouragement for a Conservative government that was determined to crush the militancy of the NUM was in the commercial interest of newspaper proprietors. As they were having to prepare for their own subsequent confrontation with the print unions, they were as keen as Thatcher to ensure the defeat of the country's strongest and most disciplined force of organised labour (and within months of the NUM's defeat Rupert Murdoch began recruiting alternative print workers for his new plant at Wapping).

Never before in my experience had the popular press been so partisan for so long. Their demolition job on the character and reputation of Scargill was unparalleled in its unrelenting ferocity. Nonetheless, leaving aside their vitriol, leading tabloids such as *The Sun*, *Daily Mail* and *Daily Express* were essential reading. They were in effect the mouthpiece for the government and the NCB. Their journalists – unlike a labour and industrial correspondent such as myself reporting for the BBC – had a hotline to influential sources of information such as Tim Bell; Bernard Ingham, the Downing Street press secretary; and David Hart, who was an adviser to both Thatcher and Ian MacGregor, and who went on to assist working miners to fund legal action against the NUM and then to form the rival Union of Democratic Mineworkers.

The media's focus in the final months on the increasing number of 'new faces' was a perfect illustration of the dynamic of an agenda-setting story line. Once the Nottinghamshire coalfield had challenged Scargill's authority and defied the strike, the popular press was only too keen to play up divisions within the NUM and to work in league with the government to drive a wedge between strikers and working miners. In the face of an ever-tightening police grip on picketing, and the failure of epic struggles such as the Battle of Orgreave to stop production in steel and other industries dependent on coal or to halt all deliveries to power stations, the government's tactic was to sit out the dispute while striving to weaken support for the strike from within the workforce. Regular announcements were made each weekend offering guaranteed wages and enhanced redundancy payments on condition miners gave up the struggle. On the following Monday mornings, television pictures, filmed from behind police lines, showed men being bussed into their pits, braving the pickets. By giving the strikebreakers hero status in their news coverage, the tabloid press helped build up interest. The momentum worked to the advantage of the government's agenda with reporters waiting eagerly each week to get the latest figures so as to chart the speed of the strike's collapse.

Unlike many other trade union leaders of his generation, Scargill had mastered the demands of news reporting on television and radio; he seized every opportunity to speak directly to his members and supporters, by-passing the hostility of press coverage. However, he had not realised the full impact of the dramatic pace of change within the news media. The workplace was no longer the only front line for settling disagreements with employers and a new arena was opening up which would have a profound impact not only on the way news was reported and presented, but also on the conduct and outcome of industrial disputes. Viewers and listeners were being offered a vast array of new services: breakfast-time television was building up its audience after being launched by BBC and TV-am in 1983; there was considerable new investment in regional television programming; local radio stations were opening up across the country, encouraging their listeners to participate in phone-in programmes; and the national newspapers, which were benefiting from increased advertising revenue, had more editorial space to give to columnists and commentators.

A rapid expansion in the output of news and current affairs required longer bulletins and more in-depth coverage; editors developed an insatiable appetite for live reporting. Up-to-the-minute stories on the miners' strike supplied a sense of urgency which producers craved. But television and radio began to turn an even harsher spotlight than the press onto abuses of trade union power. Pictures were telling the story far better than the words of newspaper journalists in what had become a make-or-break confrontation for the shock troops of the TUC. Violence which marred picket-line confrontations provided compelling television footage, hence the clamour for shots of Monday morning clashes outside pit gates where buses with their blinds drawn were taking in 'new faces' through a barrage of abuse.

A failure to understand the limitations of industrial strength was perhaps one of the NUM's fatal mistakes. Could more have been done to win public support? Solidarity on the picket-line was sometimes no match for the state's ability to exploit and manipulate the access, openness and participation offered by the electronic news media. News bulletins and discussion programmes were available at the flick of a switch morning, noon and night providing a non-stop national and local arena for information, comment and opinion. Trade union leaders who had previously shunned the media, believing they could rely solely on the movement's industrial strength, were having to come to terms with the impact of 24/7 reporting and the way powerful forces could manipulate the news agenda and influence the all-important narrative that framed the day's coverage.

While traditionally the left had been able to ignore the right-wing press and appeal directly to the membership for solidarity, such was the strength of the Thatcherite propaganda against the NUM that it became all-encompassing in the rapidly-evolving era of 24-hour news coverage. Increasingly a storyline nurtured and sustained by the tabloids was being reflected across the output of many of the new and competing outlets. A review of the morning papers had become a vital component of late-night and breakfast television programmes, offering viewers what in effect was a showcase for the day's front pages and latest editorial thinking. Inevitably headlines and pictures tended to highlight picket-line violence at the pit gates. Opinionated columnists were given free rein to adopt highly partisan positions which were then reflected in press review discussions between presenters and guests and which were often picked up later on daily talks shows and radio phone-ins, provoking further controversy. Expanded news bulletins over breakfast, at lunchtime, and in the early evening, gave correspondents extra air time to give a running commentary on the combined efforts of the NCB, government and police to thwart the pickets and break the strike.

Scargill was no mean opponent in reaching out to journalists and often, single-handed, he managed to command the attention of Fleet Street and the radio and television newsrooms. But his skill in projecting himself masked the failure of the miners' union to devise a communications strategy to counter the far superior news management being orchestrated on behalf of the government by Whitehall press officers, public relations advisers and advertising consultants. Scargill's repeated declaration that the media should be regarded as the enemy played into Thatcher's hands. Reporters were simply not welcome in numerous pit villages and such was the hostility towards television crews that they had little alternative but to seek protection behind police lines where they had a greater chance of obtaining the all-important footage of the latest 'new faces' abandoning the strike.

Once corralled in this way, television crews and photographers were as limited in what they could observe as embedded reporters were in the Iraq War. Radio and television coverage of the latter stages of the miners' strike provided a foretaste of what has become an Achilles heel of the modern news media. If opportunities to take pictures are restricted and there is a dearth of new information, broadcasters may find they have no alternative but to live with a degree of distortion rather than have nothing else to offer listeners and viewers. Given the increased competition, constant demand for new images and ever-tighter deadlines, it is no longer an option for a reporter to say that nothing has happened. Come what may, news bulletins have to be updated.

I quite accept that the media could have done far more to reflect the positive side of the 1984-85 dispute and the breadth of support for the miners and their families from across the country and internationally, whether it was donations, street collections, deliveries of food, clothes and toys or countless other acts of solidarity. However, help often had to be given without public recognition for fear of attracting the attention of the police, and the organisers of relief efforts did not always want their sometimes clandestine endeavours to be publicised.

A lasting, positive legacy of the troubled relationship between journalists and NUM activists – and the comparable anger and distrust among printworkers caught up in the 1986 Wapping dispute – is that trade unions usually go to inordinate lengths to avoid alienating reporters, photographers or television crews assigned to cover a strike. Disputes involving firefighters, health workers, junior doctors and many other public sector groups have all provided telling illustrations of media awareness and a recognition that giving thought to the depiction of workers in struggle can help win over public sympathy.

Firefighters have understood that television correspondents seize the chance to finish off their reports with a piece-to-camera filmed outside a fire station. Hence the brazier should always be well alight; the flames help light up the shot; and standing around in a dignified way would be firefighters carrying placards in support of their wage claim. The Fire Brigades Union had learned a valuable lesson: let the pictures help tell the story. Junior doctors and other health professionals have deployed the same understanding of the power of images. Whenever possible nurses on strike wear uniforms when marching with placards or lining up outside hospitals. Junior doctors in their white coats, with stethoscopes around their necks, were an eye-catching sight as they paraded in High Streets and shopping centres collecting signatures for their petition forms. Posters urging motorists to toot their horns in support were rarely ignored.

In applauding the advances that the trade union movement has made in improving its relationship with the news media, I in no way seek to diminish the sacrifices made by mineworkers and their communities in their year-long struggle against the forces of the state that were mobilised against them by the Thatcher government. The decade I spent reporting industrial and trade union affairs had a profound effect on my outlook and, without doubt, the pit dispute was the most momentous assignment in a sixty-year career. Reporters rarely indulge in soul-searching but I freely admit that what has troubled me most of all was coverage of the miners' struggle and the minimal editorial scrutiny of the subsequent ruination of their once great industry. Although industrial and labour reporting commands nothing like the attention it once did, I hope the 35th anniversary of the strike will encourage a reflective mood on the part of the media and a recognition that any thoughts which journalists might have harboured at the time about the Conservative government's good faith towards the future of the coal industry were tragically misplaced. I share the conclusion reached by the authors of *Media Hits The Pits* that the role of the mass media 'was not itself decisive to the final outcome' of the 1984-85 strike, but I do think that if the media's near-unanimous narrative had not been so hostile to the NUM and had instead done more to challenge the government, then Thatcher might well have been forced to reach a negotiated settlement.

Lesbians and Gays Support the Miners – Solidarity Forever!
Ray Goodspeed

30 June 1984 – Lesbian and Gay Pride March. That year something extra was added to the usual mix of campaigners and community groups, and outrageous revellers. A young Gay man called Mark Ashton, an activist (and later General Secretary) of the Young Communist League, and his friend Mike Jackson, decided to shake some buckets and collect money for the miners, who had been on strike for almost four months. They were impressed by the response. £150 was raised (1984 prices!).

That evening some Lesbian and Gay (L and G) activists in the Labour movement had, quite separately, organised a packed meeting in the University of London Student Union building (ULU) where a young striking miner from the little-known Kent coalfield addressed an L and G audience. A further generous collection was held.

Mark and Mike thought that his might be an idea worth taking further. Some 35 years and a major feature film later, people all over the world are still talking about it.

Since the strike had begun in early March collections had been held on most high streets up and down the country as well as in Labour Party and trade union branches, left groups and many workplaces. Many L and G people took part in these but not always openly.

There was already a network of Lesbian and Gay groups in the Labour movement like the Labour Campaign for Gay Rights, and some trade unions had mostly informal groups trying to change union policy. In some public sector, white collar or teaching unions, a hesitant basis for a decent policy had begun to be laid. But the majority of unions, including the National Union of Mineworkers (NUM), and the national Labour Party had yet to be won to a policy of support for Lesbian and Gay rights. The biggest far left group inside the Labour Party, Militant, was completely dismissive of L and G issues. Prejudice was widespread in the movement and in some cases even leading figures in the Labour movement were openly hostile and bigoted.

Inside the Labour Party's official youth section, which was controlled by Militant, there was a group called Lesbian and Gay Young Socialists (LGYS), many of whom were also in small Trotskyist groups.

LGYS had already raised a little money and were considering how to donate it. One of their members had connections to the Communist Party in Wales, which put him in contact with Hywel Francis in the Neath, Dulais and Swansea Miners' Support Group. Things were coming together.

Mark sent a letter to the widely-read, free London Gay newspaper *Capital* announcing a meeting on 15 July at his council flat. The aim was simply to extend the principle of the existing collections into the L and G community. Eleven turned up, all men, and LGSM was formed. The 'L' was just an aspiration to begin with!

The founders were mainly a mixture of Communists and Trotskyists and some friends of Mark. Some were from LGYS and one was even still in Militant. As the group grew, it drew in a broader mixture of men and women, from lefties of every conceivable type, to people more focused on L and G campaigning or influenced by Gay liberationist ideas from the '70s. Many other people just saw LGSM's activity and joined in, often as their first experience of activism. The members were overwhelmingly in their 20s or early 30s with a minority of older activists. Many had escaped to London from smaller towns and cities across the country in order to live more openly. It drew men and women from a working class background, who may have had instinctive sympathy with the strike. However, others were simply moved by the justice of the miners' cause or saw a direct link between the attacks of the Tories, police, media and the establishment on L and G people and the concerted attacks by the state on miners and their communities. A few weeks before, the police had viciously battered miners picketing the coking plant at Orgreave. These less 'political' members often played a central and very creative role in organising the work of LGSM and the events they organised.

The group was open to people who identified as Lesbian or Gay and wanted to support the striking miners and their communities. It had no other purpose and the support was unconditional. The first planned leaflet explained the 'relevance of the miners' struggle to Lesbian and Gay Liberation'. It did not set out to win support for L and G rights in the mining communities, though, of course, they hoped it might. A resolution passed on 2 September focused the group on single-issue, practical solidarity action. There was always the danger that the group tried to be something politically wider, and a bewildering array of political and other opinions could have led in all directions. Also, any members wishing to take part in LGSM's meetings had to collect money at least once a fortnight, on top of any other work they undertook for the group. Meetings were long, inspiring, funny, and sometimes exasperating. Sharp political differences would often be discussed at length. One such dispute concerned whether LGSM should condemn the import of coal from (Communist) Poland during the strike. Mark threatened to resign if it was passed and most members backed down. However, that kind of split was rare and the main focus was never lost.

LGSM met every Sunday to receive the cash collected, and meticulously plan the collections and other work of the group. Of course, there was no texting, mobiles, email or facebook back then, so we just had to sit there, often on the floor, until everything was sorted out and carefully recorded by Mike Jackson, the secretary. Thirty-odd people would often turn up. The highest attendance was 52. And these were organising meetings, not public meetings! Various other sub-groups were also formed to organise particular tasks. From early September *Gay's the Word* bookshop (GTW) became a regular meeting place, but it became too small and from early November the meetings switched to a room in *The Fallen Angel*, a Gay pub in Islington. LGSM sent speakers to meetings and rallies all over the country. Eventually, independent LGSM groups were set up in other cities, including Manchester, Edinburgh, Leicester and Southampton.

The Bell, an 'alternative' Gay pub at Kings Cross, was a regular and lucrative collection spot, a few times every week, and outside GTW bookshop, Saturday collections were organised in shifts. But as the group grew, Gay pubs and clubs all over London were included. As more women got involved, regular collections were held at the much smaller number of Lesbian venues. Collections, usually at closing time, took the issues of the strike way beyond the usual L and G activists and right into the heart of the more commercial scene, from Lesbian venues or leather bars to drag pubs and everything between, and lots of animated discussions were had outside the venues. Very occasionally, we had a bit of celebrity assistance! Both Jimmy Somerville and Lily Savage (aka Paul O'Grady) helped.

People were generally positive, though some Gay Tories would loudly oppose us and support Thatcher. Others did not see the miners as a natural ally of Gay people and had to be persuaded of the importance of the strike. Some had very bad memories about growing up in mining areas from which they had run away to escape to London. On the other hand, some people from those areas gave support to the miners from a natural sense of class solidarity. LGSM was particularly effective in building support and answering critics in the L and G press. It became a well-known and popular part of the L and G scene in London. The community was polarised, like the nation as a whole. The question was simply – 'Which side are you on?'

At its inaugural meeting, LGSM decided to follow up LGYS's links with South Wales. They wrote offering support in August. The Support Group in Dulais already had a wide basis of support in its own area, raising money for food which was distributed, in an impressive operation of military efficiency, to over 900 miners' households strung out in small villages throughout the valleys. The women of the community, such as Hefina Headon, were central to this operation. But it was always vital to build links with other sources of support and finance, such as union branches or support groups in places as far away as London, so miners were posted around the country to try to maximise income. This money could not be allocated through the NUM as Thatcher had seized its funds and the auditors (PwC) were hunting them down.

On 6 September, three LGSM members – Mark, Mike and Robert Kincaid – finally met a representative from Dulais, Dai Donovan, and went off to a nearby café for the first chat. Later that evening, the disco at *The Bell* was halted and Dai had the unenviable task of making his first speech in a Gay pub. His sincere thanks to the L and G community were greeted by loud applause and a generous collection. The occasion was reported in *Capital Gay*. Things were taking off.

The next Sunday, Dai, together with miners Tom Jones and Ali Thomas from Dulais, spoke to a packed, cramped meeting at GTW where LGSM members heard in detail about the issues of the strike. They were honoured to have miners at an LGSM meeting for the first time, but stunned and thrilled when they were invited to visit Dulais. It was not unusual for the Dulais Support Group to invite union branches, or supporters from other areas to visit. Inviting a group of London-based homosexuals who had raised hundreds of pounds should have been just the same, except that, in the social conditions of the early 1980s, it obviously was much more. It was a moving act of solidarity that had profound consequences.

It is difficult to convey the level of oppression of homosexuals that still existed in early '80s: the discriminatory laws that applied only to male homosexual acts; the routine police harassment; the absence of any employment protection and the threat of being fired; the family law that deprived Lesbians and Gay men of their children. But the worst aspects of the oppression were the social attitudes expressed on TV, in the media and in daily life. Homosexuals were ridiculous, dangerous, disgusting and mentally ill – and were after your children. In the absence of positive role models, it was painful growing up to discover that you might be one of these monsters, and to be open was to invite ridicule and violence. There was some progress in the world of pop music, with the emergence of Gay groups like Bronski Beat, but it was still a world where even Boy George of Culture Club would not come out as Gay, and even in 1987 the introduction of Gay characters on Eastenders caused a storm in the national media. 'EastBenders!' screamed a Sun headline.[1]

That was the context in which LGSM was invited to a small, mainly Welsh-speaking, semi-rural community based around an industry famous for its rugged masculinity. When Dai reported his invitation in Dulais, there was stunned silence, and then a bit of laughter. There was no overt hostility but all sorts of prejudices and niggling concerns about men dancing together at the welfare and so on and how that might be received in the community.[2][3] However, the invitation was confirmed, and they set about organising a social programme, and accommodation in people's houses. The committee was also concerned to protect the guests from any negative comments and behaviour.

Although the mining community in Dulais was isolated from the political and social milieu of big cosmopolitan cities like London, the miners' welfare hall was a centre of education and cultural life, way beyond the most obvious examples of brass bands or male-voice choirs. Socialist and internationalist traditions were very strong. One of the leading women in the support group, Siân James (eventually a Labour MP), had been to Greenham Common Women's Peace camp, and feminist ideas were burrowing away under the surface. Nevertheless, inviting LGSM was a much bolder proposal.

On Friday 26 October 27 LGSM members, in three minibuses, nervously set out to visit Dulais. The journey down was a mixture of politics and camp, though we wondered if we should 'tone it down' when we got there. One of us with a huge red Mohican haircut had managed to put it all under a cloth cap! The vegetarians among us debated the ethics of asking for a vegetarian meal from a community reliant on food donations! Having got lost, we turned up in the early hours, too late for some of our accommodation, so many of us had to sleep on Dai's floor for the first night.

On Saturday evening, after a programme of local cultural visits, we nervously assembled to enter the welfare hall in Onllwyn filled with hundreds of people from the local community. A member, Andy Denn, was 'volunteered' to speak from the stage. After we were announced, there was a moment of silence followed by widespread and sustained applause. It was a marvellous feeling. An evening of lamb stew, a male voice choir, bingo and dancing followed. So did various respectful but curious conversations during which it actually became clear how similar we were rather than how different. For many LGSM members, this response was deeply moving and inspiring, one that many of us would not have expected in our own home towns. Mike Jackson has often said that it felt like coming home as young Gay and Lesbian people were welcomed into the heart of a traditional working class community. That was the beginning of a warm relationship that has endured for decades.

Over the course of the strike, people from Dulais also visited London and were entertained in L and G venues. The women, especially, wanted to fully experience the world that LGSM came from and build up an understanding of the issues faced by L and G people. They also wanted to have fun and laughs – and they did. The effect of LGSM's visit on local L and G people in Wales was also profound. Those who lived a secret or semi-secret life, such as Cliff Grist, a retired miner, found confidence to be more open. Teenagers from those times felt more able to come out after our visits.

LGSM members returned home fired-up to redouble their efforts to raise more money. The idea of a benefit had been discussed at the first meeting but now a very ambitious event was planned. The title of the event was 'Pits and Perverts' – a typically cheeky reclaiming of a term of abuse, often wrongly thought to be based on *The Sun* headline. A long list of L and G performers, from pop stars and comedians to drag artists was drawn up. Jimmy Somerville was a close friend of Mark Ashton, and his band, Bronksi Beat, who had just become huge international stars, agreed to headline. Celebrities donated prizes for a glamorous raffle to maximise income. It was held on 10 December 1984 at the Electric Ballroom in Camden, London. Admission was free to striking miners and many attended. It was a huge undertaking and dozens of volunteers were needed before it and on the night, but by then LGSM had more than 50 people coming to its regular Sunday meetings. Volunteers from Dulais also helped. It was a huge success.

Political speeches from miners and women from different mining communities, as well as LGSM itself, were delivered between the acts. Most memorably, Dai Donovan said, "You have worn our badge, 'Coal not Dole', and you know what harassment means, as we do. Now we will pin your badge on us; we will support you." A bucket collection of £928 was given to a woman from Kiveton Park, and £200 was donated to Hatfield Main, both in South Yorkshire, but the rest, some £4,000, was given to Dulais. A large chunk of this money was spent on a bright red van, and the committee in Wales decided, in another amazing act of solidarity, to paint the doors announcing that it had been donated by LGSM.

Meanwhile, at the 2 December meeting some women members said that they had met other Lesbians who were 'not willing to work in a mixed group', and therefore proposed a new, women-only organisation, Lesbians Against Pit Closures (echoing the Women Against Pit Closures groups in the coalfields). LAPC held regular meetings at the Drill Hall, collected at women's venues and events and twinned with Rhodesia pit in Nottinghamshire and held a benefit for sacked and victimised miners in May.

At that time many Lesbians were debating whether they should organise together with Gay men or separately as women. Almost every nominally 'Lesbian and Gay' organisation involved many fewer women than men. In LGSM, it was certainly true that women were always a small minority, averaging around 10-15% at any given time and some women said they found the style of the meetings uncomfortable. Some of the men were very supportive of LAPC, seeing a separate women's group as the same in principle as a separate L and G group. Others disliked the implication that LGSM meetings and activities were sexist or oppressive. Some women, including those in the Socialist Workers' Party (SWP) and others, continued to work in LGSM. Some worked with both groups. LGSM agreed to send a letter respecting their decision and offering support.

Early 1985 was a time of grim determination in the coalfields, as desperate poverty and relentless government and media pressure took its toll and after the hope of other unions coming out on strike had been dashed. Some miners started drifting back to work. The Swansea, Neath and Dulais area, however, stayed solid.

At a public meeting in Lambeth Town Hall on 17 January between 100 and 150 L and G people heard Ali Thomas, from Dulais, praise the loyalty and solidarity between LGSM and the mining community. A cheque for £1000 was presented to him.

A video was made to record our work and our relationship with the mining community for posterity. A number of LGSM members who were part of an L and G youth video project before the strike had produced a film called *Framed Youth – Revenge of the Teenaged Perverts* and they made use of this experience and creativity. This ultimately led to the short film *Dancing in Dulais*.

February 11 saw the first LGSM picket of a power station in Neasden in north-west London, and, soon after, an introduction to the brutality of the police. A national demonstration was called for 24 February. It was a massive turnout and the crowd was in good spirits. It included miners and their families, small children and elderly people. LGSM's now iconic banner was a focus for a much wider L and G contingent who were warmly applauded as they sang 'Solidarity Forever' from the words written on the back of the banner. In tactics which became much more common later, the police split the march at Whitehall, and sent in mounted police with batons to brutalise a peaceful demonstration. LGSM was caught up in the middle of it. One member, the most mild-mannered you could imagine, was grabbed and arrested by a mounted policeman while cowering against a wall. He was later charged, ludicrously, with threatening behaviour. The police in court told shameless, barefaced lies and he was fined £130 plus £50 costs. That evening, a shell-shocked LGSM issued a statement: 'This police attack has only served to strengthen our commitment to the miners' struggle.' One week later, the strike was over.

LGSM's second group-visit to Dulais coincided with the weekend that the strike was called off – with no settlement and no guarantees for victimised or sacked miners. It was a huge defeat. LGSM witnessed the distress, the crushing disappointment and the passionate debate and recriminations. It was painful to see. We had spent months saying, "If the miners' lose, we all lose!" but the true enormity of the defeat only became clear over successive months and years as the Thatcher government's assault on working class people continued and the left were marginalised. The Gay community were to suffer from the criminal neglect of the government in the face of the AIDS crisis and the new waves of discrimination that it unleashed. Section 28 was introduced to halt the progress towards social acceptability for 'homosexuals' and their 'pretended' families.

The dignified and poignant march back to work was unbearable to watch, but there was a strong determination to keep the support going as the mining communities were still suffering. A jumble sale on 9 March and a camp glamorous fashion show of the donated items, the 'Night of a Thousand Socks', raised £380. The total for that week was £680. A conference drawing the lessons of the strike for the Lesbian and Gay movement was held on 30 March at the London Lesbian and Gay Centre. The famous commemorative enamel LGSM badge was designed, in the style of a miners' badge, to raise more funds. There was a sponsored cycle-ride to Dulais and another group-trip to

Dulais that Easter (late April). But pub collections stopped by mid-April and the final meeting of LGSM was 21 June 1985.

However, there was one last triumph. In March, LGSM had invited people from mining communities to march with them on the next Pride March on 29 June, so it was not unexpected. Even so, the sight of a contingent of miners from South Wales marching behind the Blaenant Colliery banner at a Pride March, behind the Big Red Band (a brass band from London), was astonishing and deeply moving. Such a gesture of solidarity from (mainly) straight trade unionists had never happened before and the crowds on the march could barely believe their eyes. Even better, because of the numbers involved, the organisers agreed to let us lead the march, which we did to rapturous cheering and applause. Siân James from Dulais spoke from the stage at the end of the march. A bit of history was made.

More history was made later that year. Following LGSM's work with the mining communities, the NUM gave their support to a 'Gay rights' motion at the TUC conference in September. Their example led other unions to support it and it was passed for the first time ever. In October, at the Labour Party conference, trade union support finally led to the passing of a motion supporting L and G rights, building on the steady and thorough work of Labour Campaign for Gay Rights and against the advice of the leadership. This led to the legal reforms finally achieved under Labour governments after 1997, but even before that, it helped to establish L and G (later LGBT) people as an integral part of the trade union movement and to fight for their rights at work and in society. Most trade unions opposed Section 28 in the late '80s.

Links were maintained between the communities, and particular friendships lasted. Significant anniversaries saw visits to Dulais. A large contingent from Dulais came to

London in 1987, to the well-attended and intensely moving funeral of Mark Ashton who had died, aged just 26, one of several LGSM members lost to AIDS over the years.

In the wider movement, the memory of the LGSM story began to fade, but in 2011 a scriptwriter, Stephen Beresford, made contact with some LGSM veterans, having traced them through the *Dancing in Dulais* video on the internet. He proposed making a film based on the LGSM/ Dulais story, loosely based on interviews with the original activists in London and in Wales. He was clear that it would be a fictionalised 'comedy/drama' aimed at bringing the story to the largest possible audience. It was a risk, but we accepted it.

The result in 2014 was *Pride* a mainstream movie, made by Pathé, which was a hit all over the world, and catapulted LGSM into the limelight. We had no input into the final script or plot, though some of us had appeared as extras. The differences between the film and historical reality are clear, but both the LGSM veterans and those from Wales enthusiastically embraced it, as it captured the essence and the main political points of our collective story.

The massive public and media interest generated by *Pride* meant that both LGSM and the Neath, Dulais and Swansea Valley Support Group had to re-form, to present a united and organised response. Links were re-established and strengthened, culminating in an emotional reunion back in Onllwyn welfare, where LGSM received a sustained and emotional standing ovation. Members of both groups were involved in promoting the film internationally and we were flooded with requests for speakers in connection with the movie and the true story, both in Britain and all over the world. For a year, LGSM led almost every Pride march in towns and cities across the UK. At the Pride march through London we received a welcome normally reserved for World Cup champions as we led a trade union contingent, together with actors from the film and many of our new supporters, through the street of the West End. Our famous t-shirt is now seen everywhere and money raised from sales of merchandise has been donated to mining, trade union or related causes, especially the Orgreave Truth and Justice Campaign, with whom LGSM has close links. We are a regular feature at the Durham Miners' Gala.

The politics of LGSM/Pride has inspired and motivated an entirely new generation of young activists, both socialist and LGBT (or both!) interested in the links between sexual politics and ideas of class struggle and solidarity. *Pride* could not have been released at a better historical moment. The labour movement is waking up after decades of defeat and retreat. Small but important strikes are taking place, radicalising a new generation. In the UK many on the younger periphery of LGSM went on to form Lesbians and Gays Support the Migrants, their name a conscious tribute to ours. Other LGS(*) groups have been set up in other countries.

In December 2015, LGSM disbanded again, but a small committee preserves our legacy on our website, maintains a twitter account and deals with merchandise sales and speaker requests. Our message of LGBT liberation, working-class unity and solidarity live on.

NOTES

(1) Piers Morgan – No stereotypes were harmed in the making of this film – *Daily Telegraph* (18 Sep 2015)

(2) Tim Tate with LGSM, *Pride* (2017), p170-173

(3) Hywel Francis, (2015), *History on Our Side: Wales and the 1984-85 Miners' Strike*, (2edition) p111-112

When the long arm of the law overreaches
Morag Livingstone

There has been much written over the last 35 years about the miners' strike of 1984-85. The focus of newsprint and documentaries has often fallen on one hot summer day that is forever engrained in the minds, bodies – and in some cases the skulls – of those who were there. South Yorkshire, Orgreave, 18 June 1984. Where 95 men were arrested and charged with violent disorder or riot.

The memory of the events of that day and the call for a public inquiry are kept alive through campaigns, anniversary marches and speeches. Books have been written and films made about the miners who once thought they had a job for life in the coal industry, but a few months after Orgreave many found themselves facing a life sentence. While the case of riot against 13 of the men at Orgreave collapsed in 1985 and some compensation was paid for their troubles in 1991, the injustice lingers on. The feelings of communities who once trusted the police were summed up by one of the miners following his acquittal: "I can't forgive the police for those things. I had respect for them before the strike, but not now." [1]

A public inquiry, truth and justice for Orgreave, has been called for on numerous occasions across the decades by the community, MPs and campaigners, but denied many times by successive governments.[2]

Eye-witness accounts, police footage and the work of many journalists and lawyers over the years have shown the long arm of the law overstretched its boundaries that day. Testimony and police video confirms that violence from the miners did not start until after the police sent horses into a crowd of people taking a stand against mass pit closures.

The closures heralded by miners' leader Arthur Scargill were denied by the government at the time, only for Scargill to subsequently be proven right.

When the strike was over, the government implemented the mass closure of the mines and in turn devastated many of the UK's industrial communities. What is worse is that the government planned the closures but had no plan to rebuild. They left communities without industry or good jobs. Communities that had worked to fuel the nation found their government turned against them.

While many across the UK think the police are and should be neutral it was made obvious by the man responsible for police operations at Orgreave, Assistant Chief Commissioner Clement, that they were not. In his testimony at the trial of 13 men for riot (that subsequently collapsed) he said his only job was to ensure the lorries moving to and from Orgreave Coking Plant had smooth passage.

It is now known that the police sent horses into a peaceful crowd at Orgreave, without warning, under his instruction. ACC Clement testified that it was to move the protestors back because, based on past experience, he assumed the crowd would be violent. He brought in dogs to surround the perimeter that in the end served to restrict the safe exit of miners when the mounted police, followed by policemen with short shields and truncheons, were sent in.

The defence cross-examined the timing and order of tactical operations led by ACC Clement during the 1985 riot trial. They found his evidence inconsistent at best. Whatever the approach ACC Clement took, it is important to note that in the UK the police have a duty to act only in self-defence. They are obliged to keep the Queen's peace. Any response to public disorder should be met with proportionate force.

The violence that followed the horses meeting the crowd lasted most of the hot summer day at Orgreave. *The Independent* newspaper called it 'a breakdown of police discipline' involving 'tactical failure'.[3] But were the failures really caused by a 'breakdown of police discipline' in that field and on the streets around Orgreave Coking Plant where the Battle of Orgreave took place? While those seeking the truth have carefully examined events of the day, the answer to the question that many have asked still eludes: How could this have been allowed to happen?

This was, in part, answered by ACC Clement himself when, in response to cross examination, he mentioned an Association of Chief Police Officers (ACPO) manual of Public Order Policing. It was the first time that the defence became aware of such a manual. It transpired that the manual was classified and so not a public document. Due to this secret classification and to enable the defence sight of the relevant parts of the document, the judge first ordered that the prosecution should review the manual, find the information the defence was looking for, and issue that to the defence, but not the jury. A few days later, on request of the defence, he subsequently ruled that these sections could be submitted as evidence and hence seen by the jury.

I first heard of the manual when making my first feature documentary *Belonging: The Truth Behind the Headlines*, a film about where power lies, and connects government, media and corporate collusion across three industrial disputes over three decades and three successive governments.[4] When I started researching for *Belonging* there was a new documentary about to be released on the miners' strike *Still the Enemy Within* so I decided not to re-examine events during the miners' strike, but instead focus on the connection between three other disputes: Ineos, Grangemouth (2013); the Royal Mail, Burslem (2007-08), and News International Wapping dispute (1986-87).[5]

The police public order manual used at Orgreave was of interest as it was also the basis of public order policing during the Wapping dispute. I wrote Freedom of Information requests. I asked around. I called in favours. Nothing. The police tactics manual was a classified document, and that was that. I was, however, given a copy of ACC Clement's testimony which, as revealing as that was, contained no attachment in the form of a manual.

I heard rumours that the Home Office had sanctioned the manual for public order when it was published in 1983. Publicly I could find no mention of this – newspapers and MPs in parliament referred to it as a classified ACPO document created by ACPO after the riots in Brixton in 1981. This is important, because, if the Home Office were involved in its creation, it is arguable (depending on what was in the manual) that the doctrine of law in relation to the UK policing of public order had been changed behind closed doors and without Parliamentary scrutiny. If the Home Office had been involved, elements of public order policing during public disorder may well be unlawful from its first use to the present day. Perhaps nothing is as it seems.

When Terry Smith, a former compositor for News International who features in the *Belonging* documentary, first told me 'it's not what's in a newspaper, it's what's not in a newspaper that counts', I changed my research approach and went back over my files. [6]

First: the transcripts of the Orgreave Trial and the cross-examining of ACC Clement. He claimed he was involved in the development of the manual and the defence asked about Home Office involvement. The prosecution objected, for reasons of relevance. The judge allowed the objection. Where previously this seemed irrelevant, I now wondered why the prosecution shut this question down. If the Home Office were not involved, then would the prosecution have objected to the question? I was also told that there were rumours that the then Home Secretary had sanctioned the manual.

But did that matter when ACC Clement stated in evidence that the police operations manual was just a guide and not intended to cover industrial disputes? The prosecution also told the court: 'The manoeuvres are not exhaustive. They form the basis upon which others could be developed to satisfy local need.' Either way whatever ACC Clement's defence – if the rule of law is understood, such manoeuvres should maintain the doctrines of self-defence and keeping the Queen's peace. Those sections of the manual released to the defence showed that, contrary to ACC Clement's evidence that a warning was optional in these circumstances, the manual actually states that when horses are used 'a warning should always be given'.

Arguments over the years around not holding a public inquiry include that the police profess to have undertaken their own examination of events following the miners' strike. But what lessons were learnt when eye-witness accounts confirm that no warning was given by the police before sending in the horses at Wapping either? But was there anything in the manual to confirm that the Home Office was involved in its creation? More freedom of information requests and searches at the National Archive provided no new leads, no answers.

Much of *Belonging* was made in my spare time and, late one night, I decided to go back to Hansard, the Parliamentary record, and put in every word I could think of in the search key relating to public order. I was tired; it was 1.45 am. I typed in something I don't recall and there it was. Tony Benn speaking in 1986 about the violence at Wapping: 'Police Operations Manual – extracts of which you, Mr. Speaker, authorised me to place in the Library of the House last year....' [7]

I stared at the screen, I felt sick – and elated. The fabled manual pages were in the Parliamentary library. In the light of my computer screen, I laughed out loud. I sat back. Here the missing sections of the manual are – hiding in plain sight.

In the end, it took over six months before I got access to

Parliament to see the sections of the manual released into court as evidence in 1985. Eventually I got the call – I could come in. I was told they had had difficulty finding them as they were misfiled. The night before I went to Parliament I couldn't sleep. I kept checking my small camera was charged; that my phone had enough space to act as a back up camera if needed. My mind went into overdrive. I didn't know if I wanted to know what was in these pages after all. Surely I already knew enough. I could just walk away, leave this alone and get on with a simpler path of life. I could stop any time. I could decide not to think about Wapping, Orgreave, the guys at Royal Mail and Ineos and their families any more. I thought about preserving, not pushing, my boundaries of knowledge. I tried to convince myself that there would be nothing in it, that it would be a waste of time anyway. Eventually my mind became clear of fear. I thought about those who can never walk away because they lived through what happened at Orgreave then saw government, media and police actions repeated elsewhere in the years since. I thought of the pain in the eyes of those I'd interviewed and I wanted to see what could be proven, if I could help.

I arrived ridiculously early. When I saw the security, doubts crept in again. I turned and walked back along Westminster Bridge away from Parliament trying to decide what to do. I looked up at Big Ben. I'd already started putting a hole through everything I had learnt in my life to date. I was struggling ... It's not what's in a newspaper that counts. I stood on the bridge with two conflicting views of the world in my head and at that point I still didn't know which one was right. I thought of how similar the stories from trade unionists across the decades were about government, corporate and media collusion. I thought of all those I'd met, from Orgreave to Grangemouth, who despite both being attacked by their employer and government, despite facing serious prison sentences, and despite being personally vilified in the media, still told me their version of events and trusted me not to abuse that trust. I couldn't let them down because, despite everything that had happened to them, they still believed the truth will out. Whatever was in those documents, I wanted to know. I walked into Parliament unsure which version of the 'truth' I would come out with.

I was handed two A4 envelopes. I opened the one that looked like an original. I scanned the pages. There was nothing there on mounted police. The word 'incapacitate' was underlined in relation to short shields, but I didn't, at that time, have the knowledge to understand why. Gutted. Just 10 pages. Nothing on the use of truncheons or deploying mounted police. I decided to note down what was there anyway so I could ask people with more knowledge. I asked if I could photograph or film the pages. The response, with a smile: "I am off to make a cup of tea, I'll be back in about 10 minutes. Do you want one?" My camera was out before the door closed. I photographed every page; still despondent, I reached for the other envelope marked 'COPY'. I photographed those pages too. I froze. I reached for the original and placed it next to the copy. I carefully counted the pages of each. There were two extra pages in the copy version. One headed 'Mounted Police' and the other 'Use of Truncheons'. I collected myself and photographed these pages carefully. I set up my camera and filmed, not really taking in what I was reading. That 'incapacitate' was underlined still didn't make sense.

It was early 2016, and I'd been working on making *Belonging* since November 2013, when David Cameron accused Stevie Deans, a trade union convenor at Grangemouth, for nearly bringing down the Scottish petrochemical industry. My first job was in the oil industry and I knew someone in Stevie's position wouldn't have that much power.

Walking back to London Waterloo to catch my train, I once again stopped and looked back at Parliament. They knew. They know. Overwhelming sadness. The police lied. The government lied. The injustice.

I didn't know what to do next. On their own the two extra pages verified what I didn't want to be true. But it wasn't enough to determine whether or not the Home Office had been involved in the creation of the manual, and, if so, had they sanctioned it? Because if they did then the implications for UK policing of public order stretch further than the end of an individual's truncheon and Orgreave. Again I wondered at how a police disorder situation such as Orgreave or Wapping could have come about.

Having worked in an office for 15 years, prior to becoming a journalist, I knew that when new processes are developed, there's a file of record showing how. It's generally kept so that decisions can be justified later. If the Home Office had been involved, I reasoned there may be a file and, due to the passage of time, that file should be at the National Archive. There was: Public order training: Police Training Council, Public Order Training Steering Group and Public Order Liaison Group; drafting of Association of Chief Police Officers (ACPO) manual on community disorder tactical options. 1982 – 1983.

I spent a number of days going through the files. I cried over them, because of them. I felt my mindset shift, and all that I believed before, about government working for the greater good, crumbled away. Despite what Clement had stated in court the files confirmed that the manual did cover all public disorder events. I met with an Orgreave barrister to hand over a copy of all the files and asked about the underlining of 'incapacitate'. I was advised it was significant because the manual seems to give a general authority to incapacitate anyone that is present. That is, the manual goes beyond the self-defence doctrine.

Also in the files are the background workings and drafts of the manual. At the 1985 trial the prosecution did not pull out the following paragraphs which served as a reminder to the police of their duty:

> 2. *Use of force generally. There is a clear and absolute duty on police to enforce the law and maintain the Queen's peace. In carrying out this duty there are occasions necessary to use force. But the use of force is justified only if it 'is reasonable in the circumstances in the prevention of a crime, or in effecting or assisting in the lawful arrest of offenders or suspected offenders or of persons unlawfully at large'(section 3(1) of the Criminal law Act (1967))*
>
> *1.13: Nothing in this guideline affects the principle to which section 3 of the Criminal Law Act 1967 gives effect that only minimal force necessary in the circumstances must be used.*

Like the police statements made at Orgreave, just because it is written, does not mean it is so. Orgreave. Wapping. The words of Tony Benn's Parliamentary speech came back to me:

> *…under which peaceful demonstrators may be attacked without provocation by mounted and foot police, and disabled by the use of truncheons. As a result of that police action, a number of people have been injured and a number of arrests have been made.*

So focused was I on the statement that Tony Benn had put parts of the manual in the library, I missed the significance of what he said. The files at the National Archive also proved that the Home Office was involved in the creation of the manual. As set out in *Belonging*, the Home Office file showed it was they who instigated a new manual of Public Order. They who ran and hosted the meetings and even held a celebratory drinks party with the Home Secretary when it was near completion (ACC Clement's name does not appear on the invitation list in the file). In his speech, the Home Secretary acknowledged the importance of manual and hard work of the liaison committee. However, a short while later when the Home Secretary and his advisors had a chance to review the content of the manual, they asked for changes.

It was also recommended that the Home Secretary 'distance himself' from the manual by just giving his general authority to it. Concerns were raised and changes requested by the Home Secretary's office. The file also shows that while the original intent of the Police and Home Office working committee was to create a police operations public order manual classified no higher than 'confidential', it appears from the files that this was changed in the final weeks before publication to security 'Classified' following the office of the Home Secretary conducting its review. The Home Office was concerned not only about the creation of the manual and its content but that 'Home Office involvement would one day become public'.

Those who bore witness at Orgreave deserve more than new words and analysis. They deserve the hidden truths to be examined, in public, at an inquiry so we know lessons have been learnt. They deserve to hear all sides of the truth. We all do.

NOTES

(1) This statement from Mr Jackson, one of the acquitted miners, was published in a number of newspapers when the 13 miners received compensation in 1985. This article was found in a National Archive file entitled 'Complaints – Disturbance at Orgreave Coking Plant 1985' File ref HO287/3604. It is not known what newspaper it came from but is headlined 'I can't forgive the police … I had respect before' and is article number 26 in the Media Scan

(2) More information on the Orgreave Truth and Justice Campaign can be found here: *https://otjc.org.uk/*

(3) *Independent* Newspaper editorial comment, 21 June 1985 'A Question of Order'

(4) More information on the multi-award winning documentary, *Belonging: The Truth Behind the Headlines* can be found here: *www. belonging4us.com*

(5) More information on *Still the Enemy Within* can be found here: *https:// the-enemy-within.org.uk/the-film-3/*

(6) Terry Smith was a compositor at News International. He was a witness to the police violence at Wapping and was there when the Trade Unions stopped the front page of *The Sun* showing Arthur Scargill waving, but represented as doing a Nazi salute – even giving me the original hand-written copy he had held on file for 30 years. More on the police violence at Wapping, Terry, the similarities between three disputes over three decades and conspiracy theory proven as conspiracy fact can be found in *Belonging: The Truth Behind the Headlines*

(7) Tony Benn MP, Public Order Bill, *Hansard* 13 January 1986.

After the Pits Closed
Pete Lazenby

The enormity of the effects of pit closures on mining communities is difficult to grasp, even today. My experiences as a reporter are mainly in the Yorkshire coalfield, but what has happened in Yorkshire has been mirrored in former pit communities across the UK. In Scotland and South Wales, Lancashire, Nottinghamshire, Staffordshire, Durham and the North East, the effects continue today.

Yorkshire was the biggest coalfield in the UK, representing almost one-third of the whole of the country's deep-mined coal industry. When I became Industrial Reporter on the Yorkshire Evening Post in 1974 Yorkshire had 65 deep coal mines, out of a national total of 200.

So vast was the Yorkshire coalfield that the National Coal Board (NCB) which ran the coal mining industry on behalf of the Government following nationalisation in 1948, had to break Yorkshire up into four administrative areas – South Yorkshire, North Yorkshire, Barnsley and Doncaster. Other big coal mining areas, such as South Wales and Scotland, were single administrative areas.

By the time of the strike against pit closures in 1984, the number of pits had fallen to about 50 in Yorkshire, but it still remained the biggest coalfield in the UK.

Each pit employed on average 1,000 mineworkers. On each mineworker's job depended at least twice as many others in related industries, ranging from engineers manufacturing the machinery used in the pits to the rail workers who transported the coal.

Then take into account the small shops and other businesses in the mining communities which were as dependent on the existence of the pit as were the miners who worked there, and their families.

Although this book marks the 35th anniversary of the start of the strike against pit closures in 1984, the single key year in terms of closures is 1993 – the Tories' final onslaught on the nationalised coal mining industry prior to privatisation of the 19 pits which were to remain, though even their existence was short-lived in terms of the history of the coal mining industry. The last two pits to close were Hatfield Main in Doncaster in summer 2015 and Kellingley Colliery in West Yorkshire in December that same year.

After the strike ended in 1985 the Government began to implement its hit list of pit closures – a hit list whose existence it had denied throughout the strike. From 1985 to 1992 125 deep mines were closed with the loss of 125,000 mineworkers' jobs.

The effects on employment were to a small extent mitigated initially, because at least some of the mineworkers whose pits had closed could be absorbed into those which remained. And even in the 1980s new pits were still opening – the huge Selby coalfield was still under development. It was the largest single coal mining development the world had seen, with an expected eventual workforce of 4,000. Mineworkers from closed pits flocked to work there.

But when the last great tranche of 31 Tory-imposed pit closures was announced in 1992, the sponge which had soaked up sacked miners was becoming saturated.

The effects of those closures on coal mining communities in 1993 has been well documented: the financial sharks moving in to 'advise' sacked mineworkers how to 'invest' their redundancy money; the gradual breakdown in discipline among young men who had never experienced the solidarity and responsibility of working in an environment in which one man's life depended on the actions of another; and later the growth of drug use.

Some former coal mining areas received regeneration

grants from Europe, a fund established to invest in alternative industries to replace both the coal and steel industries. Regeneration met with mixed success, and provided no replacement for the relatively well-paid jobs provided by the coal mines.

But in some former coal mining communities today there has been a particularly nasty development. They have been targeted by an industry which emerged years after the huge wave of pit closures of 1993, and long after the 1984-85 strike – the online retail sales industry.

The industry operates on a simple formula. Cut out the high street retailer by piling a warehouse full of goods and invite the computer-using public to buy direct from the warehouse at a lower price than the high street shops. And use cheap labour. The industry thrives on the exploitation of non-unionised labour. One practice is the use of the zero-hours contract.

Zero-hours contracts are pretty simple. When a worker is needed he or she is told to work, and is paid a pittance, sometimes even less than the national minimum wage. If the worker is not needed he or she is told not to come in to work, and is not paid. If an employee turns up for work and none is available, he or she is sent home, again unpaid.

Zero-hours contracts are not a new phenomenon. For decades before Britain's docks were unionised, dockers would turn up, crowding the dock gates, hoping they would be chosen for a day's work. The lucky few would be chosen. The rest would be turned away. In effect Britain's zero-hours contract operators have managed to bring back to life a version of that appalling system of exploitation from Victorian times.

Despite employing tens of thousands of workers in the UK today, the workers in the majority of huge warehouses where goods are stocked, packed, and from where they are distributed, are not unionised. There are no troublesome shop stewards raising issues of health and safety; no union activists checking that statutory wages are being paid.

For all these reasons the online sales industry is almost perfect for the greediest, most exploitative and most ruthless of employers. Perhaps the only alternative system with more advantages for the employer is slavery.

So how does this affect former coal mining communities?

ASOS, an online clothing retailer, is one of the big names in the industry in the UK. It set up a warehouse at the pit head in the former mining community of Grimethorpe, outside Barnsley.

For a century Grimethorpe depended on its coal mine. The pit was sunk in 1894. It employed more than 2,000 mineworkers. It was renowned in the wider world for its famous brass band. It was shut by the Tories in 1993 despite the heroic efforts of the Women Against Pit Closure movement, who established a long-running protest camp at the pit gates opposing closure – one of four women's camps in Yorkshire, with three more in Lancashire, Durham and Staffordshire.

Today the ASOS warehouse employs almost 4,000 workers – twice as many as the colliery did in its heyday. I say warehouse, but workhouse might be more appropriate, because the stories which have emerged from the place are horrific.

Here are a few of them:

– Because it takes too much time to walk to distant toilets, workers have to urinate in water fountains.

– They are subjected to regular body searches. Workers are spied on by an increasing number of CCTV cameras, and are made to remove their shoes and socks if they trigger a security alarm when they leave work.

– The warehouse has a shocking safety record. Between 1 January 2014, and 3 November 2016, 999 ambulance crews were called 120 times to the warehouse to deal with cases which included falls, back injuries, fits and even suicide bids.

– General union GMB is attempting to unionise the warehouse's workforce, but employees have been warned by managers and supervisors that anyone joining a union would find his or her job in jeopardy. Sacking a worker for joining a union is unlawful. Yet despite the threats some courageous workers who joined the union anyway are a valuable source of information as to what goes on inside.

Grimethorpe is not the only former mining community to suffer invasion by the on-line sales industry. The pit-head at Shirebrook, in the Derbyshire coalfield, is now home to one of the most grasping and greedy on-line sales employers imaginable, even by the low standards of the online sales industry – Sports Direct.

Like Grimethorpe, Shirebrook was solid during the 1984-85 strike against pit closures. Also like Grimethorpe, it was shut down during the final major wave of 31 pit closures in 1993 prior to privatisation of the remains of the industry.

Now a huge Sports Direct warehouse, similar to ASOS's operation at Grimethorpe, occupies Shirebrook's pit head. Working conditions inside are little different from those at ASOS.

Indeed, conditions were so appalling that in 2016 Sports Direct's boss, multi-millionaire Mike Ashley, was summoned to appear before a Commons Select Committee to answer for the way the warehouse workers were treated. Treatment included regular body searches when staff left work. The searches were carried out after shifts had ended when staff were not being paid. The time spent on the search process meant that the workers' wages fell below the statutory minimum wage.

Inside the warehouse workers were subjected to a 'six strikes and you're out' system for 'offences' such as being off ill or spending too long in the toilet. One pregnant woman employee was so afraid of taking time off that she gave birth in the toilet. Many of the Sports Direct workers were supplied by employment agencies, who took a cut of their wages. Jobs at the warehouses are a far cry from the relatively well-paid employment provided at Grimethorpe and Shirebrook collieries.

Sharlston Colliery

Sharlston colliery, near Wakefield in West Yorkshire, was sunk in 1873 and 100 years later employed 1,200 mineworkers. The community which surrounded the pit – like most other communities which grew up around collieries across the UK – existed for one reason: the pit. The pit was the sole source of employment. It was the bedrock of the local economy. With the closure of the pit, the community of Sharlston, with its 5,000 or so residents, lost its reason for being there.

I first came into contact with the mining community at Sharlston during the 1974 strike. For those too young to remember, the strike was over pay. The miners were up against not only the National Coal Board, but also the Tory government of Prime Minister Ted Heath.

As coal stocks at power stations ran out there were nationwide power cuts – coal was the source of more than 90 per cent of the UK's electricity supplies at that time. Heath ordered the introduction of a three-day week. All but essential industries had to shut down for two of the five days of the working week (incidentally, newspapers were considered an essential industry, as Heath needed to keep the right-wing Press's daily doses of anti-mineworker propaganda spewing forth).

There were power cuts.

Heath eventually called a general election under the slogan 'Who runs Britain?', the inference being that the contest was between the Tory Government and the National Union of Mineworkers. The electorate gave its answer. Heath lost, Labour was elected, and the miners' justifiable pay claim was met.

Ten years later I returned to Sharlston during the 1984 strike against pit closures. Its miners solidly supported the strike.

Sharlston was one of the collieries shut down in the last swathe of pit closures in 1993 prior to privatisation of the industry by the Tories. Shortly before it was closed, the taxpayer had invested around £12 million in developing new coal reserves at Sharlston. The reserves were abandoned, along with the new machinery which had been installed – such was the insanity of Tory economics which was applied to the deep coal mining industry. Even today it is difficult to get to grips with such economic madness. Only when the Tories' true intention is understood does it make sense – the destruction of the trade union movement in Britain, and in particular the National Union of Mineworkers.

The closure of Sharlston after 120 years of producing the nation's main source of energy killed the surrounding community. There was no other employment. The Kibble – the pit's mineworkers' social club – survived for a number of years after the closure but is now also gone. I had enjoyed many a pint there. The pit head was flattened, the shafts filled in, and the only reminder that a pit once existed there is a halved pit wheel erected as a monument by the side of a road leading into the village.

This year, 2019, 35 years after the end of the strike against closures, and 26 years after Sharlston colliery's winding engines fell silent, I returned to Sharlston to meet former mineworkers who were sacked in 1993 – Mick Appleyard, who had been Sharlston's union delegate to the Yorkshire Area Council of the NUM, Charlie Livingstone and Mick Wilkinson.

I worked with the three throughout the 1984-85 strike as a member of a miners' support group – picketing, marching, taking part in street collections, running benefit concerts.

After Sharlston closed in 1993 Mick Appleyard was given a part-time job working for the NUM. Today he still has the job. His role is to help former miners make claims for compensation for illnesses suffered as a result of working in the coal mining industry. He is now 75. Mick Wilkinson, who is 64, trained as a fork lift truck driver but the job did not last long. Charlie Livingstone, 68, has not worked since the pit was shut. All three uncomplainingly suffer medical ailments brought on by their work at the pit.

Charlie, who is Scottish, is a former soldier. "I did two stints at the pit, 27 years altogether," he said. "My first stint was at South Kirkby (near Pontefract in West Yorkshire). Then I joined the army – the First Battalion of the Somerset and Cornwall Light Infantry. I did six years, mainly in Northern Ireland. I did three or four tours. I was there about eight months before the Troubles started in 1969. I came out in 1975 and went to Sharlston."

Charlie gained a modicum of fame during the 1984-85 strike. Away from the pit he was a musician, singing, and playing the guitar. One song he sang was a battle-cry to miners such those in Nottinghamshire who did not strike. Its title is 'Get Off Your Knees'. The song was recorded on vinyl, and was sold to raise money for the hardship fund at the pit. Back at work at Sharlston after the strike Charlie was a headings man, which is heavy work, such as installing metal arched girders to secure the pit roof.

"It was hard work, which is why these are falling to bits now," he said, pointing to his knees. He's just had one knee replacement operation, and has been told he will have to wait six months for the second. He also suffers arthritis in his back.

"Since the pit closed I haven't done anything work-wise.

There was no work at all. There were zero-hours contracts even then but they wanted younger people. No-one over 45 or 50 had a chance." Charlie was 52 when the pit shut. "Sharlston was a family pit, but it wasn't just Sharlston, there were a dozen around here within a two mile radius."

He said that the effect of the pit closure was generational. "It wasn't so much just the guys who got finished at the pit," he said, "it was the families. Normally when a miner goes down the pit his son follows him, and his grandsons. But after that there were no jobs, just tuppence 'a'penny jobs. So today they hang about on street corners. It's terrible."

Mick Appleyard said: "After the pit closures, a few years after, they started to build this container base, because they'd got what they wanted, a low-wage economy, terrible wages, and people started coming in from Europe who'd work for even less, loads of them. Three quid an hour goes a long way in Poland, or Romania."

Charlie is married with a son who is unemployed, a daughter, four grandchildren and a great-grandchild. One effect of the Sharlston closure was that Charlie, and a lot of miners of his generation who were family men, but with no jobs, took on new roles as minders of their grandchildren, enabling the mothers and fathers both to work.

"My daughter works in a liquorice factory in Pontefract," he said. "She had to be there for five years before they made it permanent, a proper job. It was zero hours, and it took five years for her to be set on. They're not going to set people on if they can get them on zero hours contracts." Charlie looked after his daughter's kids, taking them to school, collecting them while mum and dad were at work.

Another effect of the closure has been to drive young people out of the village. "A lot of the young people have buggered off," said Charlie. "They had to move. You have to travel to get work."

With his grandchildren growing up, Charlie's job

minding them has dried up. "I do a lot of fishing," he said.

Mick Wilkinson went down the pit straight from school in 1970 – Ackton Hall, at Ackworth, next door to Sharlston. He ended up at Sharlston when his own pit closed soon after the strike. But during the strike he'd always picketed with the Sharlston miners. His is a similar story to Charlie's but starts with an injury suffered at the pit. He'd done heavy, physical jobs underground.

"When I finished I had a slipped disc," he said. "I was laid up for about a year. After that, when I got right I went on some training courses and got a forklift licence. But there wasn't a lot about. After that there was nothing. That was it. There was nowt in Sharlston."

Mick is married and has an adult son and daughter. Like Charlie, he took on a role minding his grandchildren so both parents could work. "My son married a lass from Huddersfield and lives over in Heckmondwike," he said. "He went away to work. He works for a firm that sells building materials. He's got a good job. My daughter Emma works at a garden centre. We've got three grandchildren. The eldest grandson is 18. He got a football scholarship and is at college. He'll be going to university in Leeds. My granddaughter is 15, 16 this time, and is sitting all her exams this year. She's hoping to go to Wakefield College. She's good at art and design. I looked after the grandkids so the kids could go to work. I used to do that, taking them to school."

Charlie joined in: "We both did it." "Now that the grandchildren don't need looking after," Mick said, "I go to rugby, and I like reading."

Mick Appleyard hasn't stopped working since the closure. He's been a political and trade union activist all his adult life. When the pit went he was approached by Ken Homer, one of the Yorkshire Area NUM officials, and was asked if he would take on the job of helping and advising miners on claiming compensation for illnesses relating to their work, many of them respiration-related, such as emphysema, bronchitis and pneumoconiosis, but also others such as vibration white finger, an extremely painful condition resulting from years of using vibrating machinery.

"I carried on working for the union part-time. I do a lot of claims for injuries. Tomorrow I'm going to a hospice to see an ex-miner who's dying. He's a pneumoconiosis man. There'll be some funeral money."

His job involves covering the old North Yorkshire Area of the National Coal Board, which is in fact mainly West Yorkshire, which had been dominated by coal mines, with pits around Wakefield, Pontefract, Castleford, Leeds and Huddersfield, and later the Selby coal field.

"When I took the job in 1993 it stretched from the other side of Leeds to the potash mine at Baltby, outside Whitby on the Yorkshire coast," he said.

Mick runs regular surgeries where ex-miners meet him to get help and advice. But there is even an international aspect to the work. After the 1993 round of pit closures hundreds of miners emigrated. The skills of British miners were in great demand in countries such as Australia and New Zealand. Mick said: "What had happened was, places like Australia were crying out for them to go. British miners could operate long wall mines. All the Yorkshire pits had long wall faces. Over there they'd never operated long wall faces." A long wall face involves the driving of two tunnels or roadways, parallel to each other, deep underground. When the coal seam is reached the tunnels turn at right angles towards each other and link together, exposing a long coal face. The coal face at the last deep coal mine in the UK to close, Kellingley, was around a quarter of a mile long.

As time passed the emigrant miners developed ailments which originated from their earlier work in the Yorkshire coalfield. Word spread to them of Mick's new role. "Honestly, I've had calls from Australia, New Zealand, Malta, Cyprus, America, about claims for bronchitis, emphysema, COPD (chronic obstructive pulmonary disease), white finger. These were from Yorkshire ex-miners. My name just got around," Mick said.

Mick himself still suffers pain from a back injury suffered when he was an underground worker. As a result of the injury he was transferred to a job on the pit top at Sharlston.

"I've got a spinal injury which I got at work and six years ago it got worse. I've got arthritis in my right arm where I broke it. Everything gets broken at the pit," he said.

The three ex-miners have to be prompted to talk about their injuries – they're not moaners, and conversations with them are peppered with pit humour and laughter.

But there's also concern about the wider community of Sharlston, or New Sharlston, which was the name of the village built around the colliery. Drug use and alcohol abuse has become a problem in many former coal mining communities, and Sharlston is no exception. It doesn't involve ex-miners, but is affecting the generations who have grown up in the communities since the closures – that is to say, those who didn't leave their communities in their desperate hunt for work. Generations of young people, young men, who would have followed their fathers down the pit, live aimlessly, as Charlie put it 'standing on street corners'.

When the coal mines went, so did the discipline and solidarity involved in working in them. It has left a generation of young people in former mining communities vulnerable, and in some cases easy prey for drug dealers offering a temporary escape from the dreary reality of everyday existence.

Mick Appleyard said: "It's happening all over, and not just in former mining communities. Look anywhere where an industry has disappeared. Look at Hull and Grimsby, now the fishing's gone."

The village of New Sharlston used to bustle and thrive. Sharlston Working Men's Club was a popular venue for nights out. Surrounded by a community of 1,000 miners and their families, there was no shortage of custom. "It was a big club, live entertainment, cheap beer, always packed," said Mick Appleyard. "If you didn't get in before 7pm you didn't get a seat."

The Club was run by an elected committee. Once the pit had gone, along with the 1,000 wages it generated, and as the community thinned out as families left, the packed nights of miners and their families enjoying a good night out became a thing of the past. It eventually faced closure. "A local guy took it over," said Mick Appleyard. "He turned it into a sort of sports club. There's no committee. It's nowhere near as busy as it was." Mick Wilkinson said: "It's nowt like it was. Folk don't go out like they used to."

One mystery at Sharlston lingers on – the disappearance of the Sharlston NUM branch banner. "It was in the club, The Kibble," said Mick Appleyard. "Someone was supposed to come from the union office in Barnsley to collect it. They didn't turn up, and the banner just disappeared. I've got the poles and the wheels, but no banner." Finding the banner would do something to preserve the memory of Sharlston, its miners and its community.

Hatfield Main

The miners at Hatfield Main colliery at Stainforth, near Doncaster, and their families, were treated even more appallingly than at many other pits in the 1993 round of closures, and the effects of what happened are still being felt today.

Hatfield went into production in 1916 during a period of intense pressure to turn coal to fuel the First World War.

In the 1970s it employed 1,700 men, later falling to 1,300. It was an unusual pit in that it wasn't based on a single pit community. Its miners came from five surrounding communities – Hatfield, Dunscroft, Stainforth, Warrens and Thorne. There's also a description of Hatfield as a 'gypsy pit'. It employed miners originally from Scotland, the North East, Ireland and elsewhere, and they included union activists who had been blacklisted in other coalfields. They got jobs at Hatfield by changing their names.

It was shut down in 1993 in the last wave of Tory pit closures before privatisation. The miners were sacked, but the pit was 'mothballed'– fully maintained with the intention of it being placed in private hands. But Hatfield miners had a reputation. Pits in the Yorkshire coalfield have often been described as 'militant'. It's a loose term but pretty accurate. Arthur Scargill once said when he was President of Yorkshire Area of the National Union of Mineworkers: "If by saying 'militant' they mean 'effective,' that's fine by me." But the four areas into which the coalfield was divided had different degrees of militancy. Doncaster area had the reputation of being the most militant of the four.

Mick Lanaghan, who worked at Hatfield Main for 11 years until a spinal injury invalided him out, or 'basically buggered me up for life,' as he puts it, said Hatfield was the most militant pit in the militant Doncaster area. That's quite a claim, and might be contested by former miners from some of the other Doncaster pits. But the actions of Hatfield miners suggest that he's right.

During the 1984-85 strike it was Hatfield miners who organised a convoy of cars and vans on the M1 motorway, then held a 'snap break' – snap being a bite to eat – stopping the vehicles on the motorways, blocking all three lanes and causing traffic mayhem. It was the Hatfield miners who did the same thing on the Humber Bridge.

It was Hatfield miners who felled lamp-posts on the

roads approaching the pit to stop police vans or a scab bus getting through. So the claim about militancy has veracity.

In 1994 the pit was re-opened as a private operation as the Hatfield Coal Company Ltd. But none of the original Hatfield miners who were sacked in 1993 was allowed to work there. They were effectively blacklisted.

Mick Lanaghan said: "We had a national reputation for militancy. When it re-opened as a private colliery they kicked the union off the site and employed men from other pits. They even bused miners in from Nottinghamshire."

So unemployed miners living in the villages surrounding the pit were denied jobs, while miners from elsewhere – including Nottinghamshire, where most miners betrayed their union and worked throughout the 1984-85 strike – were brought in to work the re-opened pit.

The re-opening of the pit ironically had a detrimental effect on the communities around Hatfield, said Mick Lanaghan. Because the pit was working again, the communities around the pit were not eligible for grants which could have helped them. "Because we had a colliery working we could never get a penny out of regeneration funds. Coal production did not stop until 2015," he said.

The make-up of the surrounding villages' populations changed too, with former miners and their families moving out, and other people from 'outside the borough' moving in, said Lanaghan.

Hatfield Main went through a number of private owners before it finally ceased production in June 2015. "When Hatfield finally closed you could count on one hand the number of miners there who were from the villages around Hatfield Main," said Lanaghan.

Generations of local young people who might have found work at Hatfield were denied jobs. The results of a 'no hope' future on the communities' young people could be seen in the late 1990s in statistics from local schools. The average percentage of young people leaving school in the Doncaster area with 'no attainment' – no qualifications – was 12 per cent. In schools at Stainforth it was a staggering 32 per cent.

Many young people, Mick says, have turned their backs on seeking a better future through education, and drugs are a continuing problem. "How can you tell third and fourth generation unemployed young people to go to school, go to college, get an education to get a job? They say 'what job?' They want a new pair of trainers. They see drug dealers much better off than they are. What are they going to do? There is a section of youth that sees breaking the law as the only way to do something with their lives. It's truly heart-breaking."

On a more positive note, there is hope for the local economy and the former mining communities around Hatfield Main. It involves a proposal to transform the land surrounding Hatfield Main's former pit-head into a country park, and the pit head itself into a facility with a conference centre, sports hall, museum, recreational, educational and other facilities.

A start has been made. Hatfield Main Colliery Heritage Association has already won Grade II listed protection status for the pit head gear, which still stands proud. Hatfield Main was shut down less than four years ago, and the pit head buildings are still intact, though in a poor condition.

They include the 'fan house' whose engines used to pump fresh air down one 2,500-feet deep shaft, along the underground roadways, across the coal face, back out along another roadway, until the dust-contaminated air is drawn out upwards through a second shaft. There are the two winding engine houses whose machines turned the wheels which lowered and raised men and machinery to and from the pit bottom.

If the project succeeds, the pit head buildings will be

converted into workshops and studios for artists. Mick Lanaghan said: "Pits didn't just turn out coal. They turned out artists, writers, poets. We want to provide cheap workshops and studios for them.

"We also want to formulate a way of having an underground experience through virtual reality – and even maybe a venue for couples to get married under the pit-head gear," he said, which is a remarkable concept.

"It isn't going to be easy – we know it will not be easy."

That's hopefully the future at Hatfield Main, but the past won't be forgotten either. Five years ago, for the 30th anniversary of the 1984-85 strike, the Hatfield miners installed a granite monument at the end of the pit lane where for a year they had picketed.

There's a miner's lamp engraved on it, and the words: "Hatfield NUM. Here stood the miners and families of the National Union of Mineworkers in defence of their jobs, communities, and against industrial genocide. Loyal, proud and true. Never forget – never forgive."

From the miners' strike to the gig economy
Granville Williams

In the 1970s a young journalist, Tony Sutton, worked for daily and Sunday newspapers in South Shields and Newcastle upon Tyne. Forty years later he revisited South Shields after a career which involved editing *Drum*, an anti-apartheid magazine in South Africa, and working as a journalist in Toronto, Canada.

'In the 1970s,' he observed, 'the town of 75,000 boasted high-paying jobs in shipbuilding and coal mining. Its last-remaining slums had been demolished, major roads were being built and new factories developed. And King Street, South Shields' main thoroughfare, reflected that prosperity.'

When he returned to South Shields in 2016, he was shocked by the way the town had deteriorated. King Street, 'the once bustling thoroughfare that furnished the dreams of an affluent society is now a nightmare of austerity. Many storefronts are empty, their windows displaying stark 'For Sale' and 'To Let' notices. The businesses that remain are mainly charity outlets, betting shops and pound stores for cash-strapped customers, while those that cater for the wealthier have decamped to big-box citadels elsewhere.'

The rot set in when Margaret Thatcher arrived in Downing Street late in May 1979. 'Her war on unions, especially the mine workers, together with economic policies that encouraged the offshoring of jobs, saw the collapse of Tyneside's major industries. Eleven years of Tony Blair's neoliberalism, from 1997 to 2007, continued Thatcher's work, the area hitting rock-bottom at the end of the 20th century when South Shields had the highest unemployment rate in Britain,' Sutton writes.

The social and economic consequences have been dire.

'The pre-Thatcher '60s generation knew their basic dreams would almost certainly see fruition: job-for-life security and regular pay rises would elevate their families into comfort, if not outright prosperity,' Sutton observes. 'That was the social contract developed after the end of World War II: Work hard and contribute to society, then society will take care of you. That contract died when Thatcher broke the miners' union in 1984-85. After that, it was everyone for themselves.' [1]

That last phrase is a grim echo of Thatcher's political philosophy. 'There is no such thing as society,' she had famously claimed in an October 1987 *Woman's Own* interview.

The South Shields scenario is replicated across Britain's older industrial towns – the places in the North, the Midlands, Scotland and Wales once dominated by industries such as coal, steel, textiles and engineering – which are a substantial part of the UK, accounting for around a quarter of the population.

Some basic facts bear repeating. The gap between rich and poor in Britain was at its narrowest in the 1970s, a decade when trade unionism was at its strongest.

In 2019 there is an obscene gap between those flaunting great wealth and working people battered by austerity and privatisation. Thirty-five years after the year-long miners' strike, it is now clear how decisive that struggle was. Britain is now riven by deep divisions with millions of people experiencing poverty, poor housing and precarious work with low-wages or zero-hours contract conditions.

But this reality, with rare exceptions, isn't reflected in the media. Indeed, as Winnie Byanyima points out, 'The dominant narrative which goes unchallenged is that there is no connection between the super-rich and abject poverty, that you can keep getting richer and richer, and this has nothing to do with people getting poorer.'[2]

The word 'gig', once used by jazz musicians when they were hired for a performance, has now been appropriated to describe an aspect of working life. It all sounds very hip or cool but the reality is that there is now a permanent class of people who are subject to the whims of their employers. The sheer uncertainty of the number of hours people will work from day to day creates massive financial instability in their lives. Many of these are young people.

A TUC report in 2017 estimated that one in 10 UK workers – three million – now work in insecure jobs. This situation has come about as a direct result of the assault on trade unions under Thatcher, and the wave of deindustrialisation she unleashed. [3]

High-paid, full-time jobs with pensions and holidays with pay disappeared. And, of course, the values which the miners fought for in 1984-85 – jobs and the defence of communities – were anathema to Thatcher.

Working life today

The Guardian headline of 31 May 2018 was dramatic: 'Amazon accused of treating UK warehouse staff like robots.' One of the biggest UK unions, the GMB, had used a Freedom of Information request to discover that ambulances had been called out to the online retailer's UK warehouses 600 times in the past three years. [4]

One hundred and fifteen of these call-outs were to Amazon's site in Rugeley, Staffordshire, including three relating to pregnancy or maternity problems and three for major trauma. At least 1,800 people work year-round at the Rugeley warehouse, and 2,000 more can work there over the peak Christmas period.

In contrast only eight calls in total were made over the same period from a nearby Tesco warehouse of a similar physical size and where about 1,300 people work, according to another FOI request by the union.

So what's happening? Well, the first thing is that Tesco recognises trade unions, with most of its warehouse workers members of the shop workers' union, USDAW. Unions have been fiercely opposed by Amazon. It laid off 850 employees in Seattle after a unionisation campaign, and hired American consultancy firm, the Burke Group, to defeat a union drive at its Milton Keynes facility in the UK.

But that is only part of the story. To get a clear sense of what working life is like in Amazon you need to have someone who has been immersed in the experience of living and working with other people employed by the company.

This is precisely the way James Bloodworth went about drawing together the rich and disturbing material contained in *Hired: Six Months Undercover in Low-Wage Britain*.[5] His book joins a list of other titles exploring – for people fortunate enough to be in steady, well-paid jobs and secure accommodation – an invisible world of insecure employment and poverty pay. In the 21st century this list includes Barbara Ehrenreich's *Nickel and Dimed: On (Not) Getting By in America* (2001) and Polly Toynbee's *Hard Work: Life in Low-Pay Britain* (2003).

However, in contrast to these two books, written when both the UK and US economies were booming, Bloodworth writes about working life in the aftermath of the 2008 financial crisis and the years of austerity – the years which coined the term 'the gig economy'. The author points out that the UK is enjoying 'record levels of employment ... but an increasing proportion of this work is poorly paid, precarious and without regular hours.' The author spent six months living as a zero-hours worker. The first job Bloodworth took in 2016 was at the Amazon 'fulfilment centre' in Rugeley, Staffordshire. In the early days of the 1972 miners' strike, as a journalist, I went to Lea Hall Colliery in Rugeley to meet striking miners.

It was a prosperous town with, as well as the pit, two

power stations, and Armitage Shanks, Thorn Automation and Celcon factories. Lea Hall Colliery opened in 1960 and closed in January 1991 throwing 1,250 men out of work. Now the biggest employers in Rugeley are Amazon and Tesco.

Amazon came to the town in 2011. The firm's vast warehouse, the size of 10 football pitches, contains four floors. Bloodworth's job was a 'picker' which involved rushing up and down the long, narrow aisles selecting items from the two-metre-high shelves and putting them in big yellow plastic boxes called 'totes'.

These were wheeled around on blue metal trolleys before being sent down conveyor belts to be packed for delivery. On an average day he was expected to send around 40 totes down the conveyor belts.

As he rushed around he carried a hand-held device which tracked his every movement. For every dozen or so workers a line manager would be monitoring their work rate through the devices.

In this highly pressured environment with slogans and photographs plastered on the walls ('We love coming to work and miss it when we're not here') you were designated as an 'associate' not a worker and if your performance fell below the company's targets you were not sacked but 'released'.

What happened in Rugeley can be replicated in former mining areas around the country. Sports Direct's biggest warehouse, which has been compared to a 'workhouse' and a 'gulag' by Unite, is located in Shirebrook, Derbyshire, the site of Shirebrook Colliery which closed in 1993.

ASOS, the mail order company run by the global logistics giant XPO, is located near the former mining community of Grimethorpe in South Yorkshire. The GMB union highlighted the 'invasive monitoring and surveillance' at the firm with agency workers and permanent staff saddled with onerous targets to process high volumes of orders each hour, and being discouraged from stopping to drink water or use the toilet.

A common feature of all these companies offering precarious, low-paid work is a fierce resistance to trade union organisation. It is only through undercover work by reporters and writers like Bloodworth, and the work of unions like Unite and the GMB, that we have found out what goes on inside these anonymous warehouse structures.

Bloodworth's book confronts directly the tensions of immigration and class and the way these play out in Amazon warehouses and battered, deprived communities hostile to East European workers. The book also demolishes the idea that people are happy with zero-hours contracts and exposes the underside of a 'gig economy' driven by fear and coercion. He vividly describes what working life is like 'for a permanent class of people who live a fearful and tumultuous existence characterised by an almost total subservience to the whims of their employers'.

Companies like Amazon avoid paying taxes on the huge flow of goods they sell. Any strategy to tackle them means effective regulation of these global groups, and ensuring they pay taxes in the country in which they sell their goods. One stark example: a report from the Centre for Economics and Business Research revealed that independent bookshops, which are threatened by the sheer volume of books sold through Amazon in the UK, pay 11 times more corporation tax than Amazon. Bookshops are currently closing at a rate of 3% per year with the number of independent booksellers halving over the last 11 years.

We need to call time on the exploitation and misery which sustains the gig economy, and trade unions will pay a central role in making it happen. Frances O'Grady, the TUC General Secretary, makes the point well: 'We know that when workers come together in a union, they can change their workplace for the better – helping stop unfair treatment, campaigning for equality, and pushing for better pay and decent conditions.'

The assault on trade unions

How did we get to this dire situation? A succession of Tory governments in the 1980s under Margaret Thatcher tore up laws giving unions powers to protect fellow trade unionists and replaced them with repressive trade union legislation which allowed the government to sequestrate union funds, limit trade union solidarity and restrict the numbers of trade unionists picketing at any one time.

Thatcher and a group of Tories around her were contemptuous of trade unions and were prepared to use the powers of the state to destroy them. One group of workers was a particular target — the miners. Thatcher's biographer Charles Moore records how she summoned Willie Whitelaw immediately on taking office in 1979 and announced: 'The last Conservative government was destroyed by the miners' strike. We'll have another and we'll win.'[6]

Thatcher sought to avenge the miners' victories of 1972 and 1974 and prepared meticulously for what she saw as a crucial test of her power. Indeed in 1981, when she had not had time to prepare for a miners' strike, she retreated and conceded to miners' demands.

But by 1984 coal stocks were high, the police had been trained in aggressive riot control techniques, and, after an election victory buoyed up by the Falklands war in 1983, she was ready for a confrontation with the miners.

The strike began in March 1984 when the National Coal Board announced the closure of Cortonwood Colliery near Barnsley. It was a body blow to the Yorkshire miners because the pit had just had millions of pounds spent on it and miners from another pit which had just closed had been transferred to it.

The closure was the trigger for a national strike by the National Union of Mineworkers (NUM). It was not a strike about pay but about protecting jobs and communities against a devastating round of pit closures.

Dennis Skinner, the veteran Labour MP from the former mining community of Bolsover, and himself a former miner, put it well when he spoke at With Banners Held High in Wakefield, West Yorkshire, on 5 March 2015 – the 30th anniversary of the return to work by the miners after the year-long strike:

The very idea that here in Yorkshire a 59-year-old miner, one year away from his retirement, was prepared to risk losing the roof over his own family's head in order to find a job for a 16-year-old in another part of the British coalfield that he was never likely to meet. That's real honour. It was a battle about jobs and not the pocket.

18 June 2019 will mark the 35th anniversary of a pivotal event in the year-long miners' strike – the Battle of Orgreave. On that day the NUM deployed 5,000 pickets from across Britain to prevent access to the Orgreave coking works by strike-breaking lorries that collected coke for use at the British Steel Corporation mill in Scunthorpe.

It was a bright summer day, with many miners dressed in jeans, T-shirts and plimsolls, and in a relaxed mood. Against them were deployed around 6,000 officers from 18 different forces, equipped with riot gear and supported by police dogs and 42 mounted police officers.

What followed that day was a brutal confrontation by the police with the pickets. Apart from the assaults by mounted police, short-shield units indiscriminately attacked miners. Some 71 pickets were charged with riot and 24 with violent disorder. However, both the police and most media coverage placed the blame for the carnage that day on violent picketing by miners.

Establishing the truth about who was responsible for organising the police assault has become the focus of the Orgreave Truth and Justice Campaign (OTJC), a tenacious group which includes striking miners who were arrested and charged at Orgreave. The OTJC was set up in November 2012, after the Hillsborough disaster report revealed that South Yorkshire Police had fabricated evidence about their role in the disaster.

A brilliant BBC *Inside Out* programme which exposed the same role by South Yorkshire Police's use of fabricated evidence against miners arrested at Orgreave also provided another spur. The OTJC wants a full public inquiry into who planned, organised and authorised the police assaults that day.

After the miners returned to work on 5 March 1985 there were enormous repercussions. Thatcher embarked on the widespread privatisation of public utilities, the sale of council houses, an intensification of the attacks on trade unions, and the closure of pits which had an immediate, destructive effect on the social and economic structure of communities absolutely dependent on the jobs they sustained. Pit closures were part of the brutal and broader process of deindustrialisation, which threw people into unemployment and poverty. We live today with the consequences of these multiple assaults on working class communities.

In November 2018 *The Guardian* journalist, David Conn, interviewed Michael Heseltine in the context of an article he was writing about the impact of Britain's exit from the EU on the Nissan plant near Sunderland.

Conn wrote:

I asked if he conceded that his government was too brutal in these mass closures of longstanding industries. He reflected for a moment, then replied: 'Probably it was too unthinking.' He said he regrets that there was no considered policy to improve these industries – through better management, company reforms and longer-term investment. 'Unlike Germany, Japan, France, now China, there was never any stable industrial strategy. It was much easier to say 'let the market rip',' he said. [7]

Well the market did rip. Ian Jack, writing in 1987, observed:
The actual generation of wealth has moved south, as well as the spending of it. Between December 1979 and September 1986 the number of people who worked in the manufacturing industry declined by almost two million from 7,053,000 to 5,128,000. Most of the jobs lost were in Northern England, the West Midlands, Wales, Scotland and Northern Ireland.[8]

The result was the spectre of mass unemployment and disintegrating communities.

What we have lost

On 1 May 1981 280 unemployed people set off from the Pier Head, Liverpool, to march 280 miles to London. The People's March For Jobs was organised by Jack Dromey, Colin Barnett and Pete Carter to highlight unemployment in 1981 which had surged to two and a half million.

Pete Carter's son, Mike Carter, had a troubled relationship with his father and turned down his invitation to join the march. Thirty-five years later he set out to follow the original march's route. His journey took place just before the 2016 EU referendum and his book *All Together Now?* published in 2019 gives us moving and troubled insights into the contemporary condition of England.[9]

Carter walked 330 miles across the spine of England in four weeks – from Liverpool to Widnes, Salford, Macclesfield, Birmingham, Northampton, Luton, and on to London. One strand of the book is about his attempt at some reconciliation with his father. In his last encounter with him, a fortnight before Pete Carter died on the narrowboat he lived on, there had been an angry exchange. Mike 'reeled off grievance after grievance, the anger and hurt he had caused to me, my mum and [sister] Sue.' Pete replied: 'I sacrificed everything for the struggle… You don't understand.'

'The fucking struggle,' Mike said, 'it's all we ever heard. Look around you. It's all fucked. Your life's work. Was it worth it?'

These recollections are painful to read but the accumulation of detail and analysis of 'the state of England' as Mike's journey progresses is also powerful and harrowing. We see the numerous ways established structures which sustained communities and people have been jettisoned. It is a searing critique of how 40 years of neoliberalism has ruined the lives of ordinary people. He documents how in health, jobs, housing, transport, our public spaces, welfare state and sport the working class have been hammered.

In Salford buy-to-let investors 'up from the south for the day' pay cash and snap up entire streets for their portfolios and block any opportunity for local people to buy houses. In 1981, the year of the People's March, rent for a council property cost less than 7 per cent of the average income. In 2015, for a private tenancy, that figure stood at 52 per cent of average income, and in London 72 per cent.

We're reminded too of David Cameron's comments to a group of local journalists in Liverpool in 2011. He told them the relatives of the Hillsborough victims, as they continued to seek justice, were 'like a blind man, in a dark room, looking for a black cat that isn't there.' On 12 September 2012 he had to stand up in Parliament and say he was 'profoundly sorry' for the failures that caused the Hillsborough disaster and the subsequent attempts to shift blame for the tragedy onto supporters after the publication of a damning report on the events that left 96 dead.

On 29 May 1981 The People's March for Jobs arrived in London. A delegation from the march went to 10 Downing Street to hand their petition in to Margaret Thatcher. She refused to meet them. The march itself, Carter writes, 'walked triumphantly into Trafalgar Square and a hundred thousand people had greeted them with a spirit of hope – a sense that the tidal wave they'd seen heading for shore could be stopped.'

Well that tidal wave wasn't stopped and more were to follow, with the brutal consequences described above. But maybe now there are signs that people are waking up to the fact that a set of economic and political ideas – neoliberalism – which have held politicians in thrall for decades are now threadbare. We now need fundamental political and economic change to roll back the damage done.

NOTES

(1) Tony Sutton, 'Main Street, Brexitland', *Coldtype*, Issue 130, December 2016.

(2) 'Bursting the billionaire bubble', *The Guardian Review*, 9 February 2019

(3) TUC *https://www.tuc.org.uk/blogs/why-we-should-still-be-worried-about-zero-hours-contracts*

(4) Sarah Butler, 'Amazon accused of treating UK warehouse staff like robots,' *The Guardian*, 31 May 2018.

(5) James Bloodworth, *Hired: Six Months Undercover in Low-Wage Britain*, Atlantic Books, 2018

(6) Charles Moore, *Margaret Thatcher*, Vol 1, Penguin Books, 2014, p.537.

(7) David Conn, 'Will Nissan Stay Once Britain Leaves?', *The Guardian*, 4 October 2018

(8) Ian Jack, *Before The Oil Ran Out: Britain 1977-1986*, Fontana, 1987

(9) Mike Carter, *All Together Now? One Man's Walk in Search of His Lost Father and a Lost England*, Guardian Faber, 2019.

I first got to know Mike's dad, Pete Carter in 1971, when he was a building worker in Birmingham and led a tremendous campaign to get 'The Lump' off building sites, particularly Bryants. The term referred to the way building contractors would hire labourers for the day or week and they would be regarded as 'self-employed' and paid a lump sum of money for the work that they did each day or week, hence 'working on the lump'. The individual worker would be responsible for paying tax and NI, not the employer. In reality it was a dangerous working practice which meant many workers were trading off working conditions and health and safety on sites for higher pay.

In early 1972 I was contacted by David Hart, a *World in Action* producer with the ITV company Granada, who wanted to make a programme about this issue. Pete Carter and the UCATT Regional Secretary, Ken Barlow, cooperated fully and the outcome, *The Lump*, shown on 27 March 1972, was a classic WIA programme.

Prising open hidden secrets of the pit strike
Nicholas Jones

When I looked around the room at the press preview for the release of the contents of Margaret Thatcher's 1984 cabinet records, the memorable words of Tony Blair came to mind for the briefest of moments: "I feel the hand of history upon our shoulders." Here I was, in late December 2013, the only journalist at the National Archives in Kew that day who had reported the 1984-85 miners' strike, which for me had been a once-in-a-lifetime assignment. Retirements and ravages of time had cut a swathe through the once mighty corps of labour and industrial correspondents and, as their sole representative at the preview, I felt a sense of responsibility. In front of assembled journalists, many of whom were perhaps still at school or university in the mid-1980s, were heaps of the former Prime Minister's cabinet papers and correspondence. Here before us would be hitherto hidden facts explaining how 30 years earlier Thatcher had succeeded in mobilising the full force of the state to crush the longest and most violent industrial struggle of post-war years.

We were all convinced the piles of documents we were about to open would hold government secrets that would tell us more about what became an historic, year-long fight to the finish between the Prime Minister and Arthur Scargill, President of the National Union of Mineworkers. Having reported on the dispute from start to end, I could hardly wait to begin reading the small print of what had been written in secret or said in private by the Prime Minister, her cabinet colleagues, advisers and civil servants. My mind was full of unanswered questions. Who might have been misleading whom? Had miners and country been lied to during the strike? There could hardly have been a more awe-inspiring moment for a journalist who had spent the intervening three decades following step by step the slow, brutal death of the coal industry. Rather like a detective in a television drama, I thought I had a good idea where bodies might have been buried.

Younger newspaper journalists were gripped immediately by what de-classified documents were revealing about how close Thatcher had been to declaring a state of emergency in July 1984 when dockers walked out in a short-lived strike in support of the miners' demand for a blockade to halt all imports of coal. Four months into the pit dispute, the Prime Minister was within days of recalling Parliament to ask MPs to pass a new Emergency Powers Act to put the army on stand-by and prepare for 4,500 troops to take over from striking dockers. Thatcher was told in a confidential Downing Street memo that servicemen should be used only 'in a grave emergency and as a final resort when the totality of the available civilian resources is inadequate'. In the event the strike threat at ports was withdrawn after a government undertaking to stand by the dock labour scheme and maintain financial support for 4,000 surplus dockers. Speculation that Thatcher was willing, if necessary, to call in the army was a recurring and well-publicised storyline for reporters covering the strike and confirmation of this didn't stand out to me as the top headline. I was on the look-out for disclosures that would be far more revealing about the way Thatcher had micro-managed the conduct of the dispute and her success in co-ordinating an unprecedented response by police and security services to defeat the NUM.

My search was not in vain. Tucked away in correspondence was the revelation that the National Coal Board chairman, Ian MacGregor, 'had it in mind' as far back as September 1983 to close 75 pits, which in my opinion confirmed that Scargill was right all along in his claim that MacGregor had a 'secret hit list'. Of even greater interest were notes and memos charting steps the Prime Minister had taken to 'stiffen the resolve' of police forces across the country to halt the movement of NUM pickets. Thatcher's hidden hand leaped from the pages: she underlined key words, sometimes two or three times, and had written her instructions in the margins, including her advice that money should possibly be sent direct to South Yorkshire police to pay for reinforcements and police dogs deployed at the 'Battle of Orgreave'.

The more I read about Thatcher's day-to-day management of the most critical industrial dispute of post-war Britain, the greater my sense of awe at her personal command of the government machine. Shortly before the start of the strike Scargill had claimed that MacGregor had a secret plan to close 70 pits with the loss of 70,000 jobs, a claim that Thatcher would categorically deny. She and her ministers insisted time and again that MacGregor wanted to shut only 20 pits with 20,000 redundancies. The cabinet records, released under the 30-year rule, exposed the full extent of government misinformation. MacGregor had outlined his target for pit closures at a private meeting with Peter Walker, Secretary of State for Energy, six months before the start of the dispute. Several days later at a meeting in Downing Street held on 15 September 1983, Walker gave Mrs Thatcher a detailed report on MacGregor's proposals.

A cabinet office account of their conversation revealed that MacGregor 'had it in mind' for the three years of 1983-85 that 'a further 75 pits would be closed'; the first 64 closures would reduce the workforce by 55,000 and the next 11 would secure a further manpower reduction of 9,000. Thatcher ordered there should be total secrecy and agreed with Downing Street officials that under no circumstances should MacGregor's plans be revealed to the public. Peter Gregson, cabinet office deputy secretary, had advised that because MacGregor's plans were so 'sensitive' there should be no further written record of what had been said; future estimates of closures and job losses should be referred to by way of 'a short oral briefing'.

Only one copy was made of the original document mentioning 75 pit closures. At the top of the three-page manuscript was the instruction: 'Secret not to be photocopied or circulated outside the private office'. A hand-written note in the right hand corner stated: 'typed by Lillian, seen by MCS, P Gregson, FERB, one copy made and given to Sir R Armstrong (cabinet secretary)'. Only three cabinet ministers knew of MacGregor's target – Walker, Nigel Lawson (Chancellor of the Exchequer), and Tom King (Secretary of State for Employment). They would have realised that it would have been a political disaster for the Prime Minister if advice MacGregor gave as early as September 1983 ever became public. So effective was the subsequent cover-up within Whitehall that the 75-pit closure list was never mentioned again in cabinet papers, nor was it ever referred to during the year-long pit strike. Public confirmation of its existence would have allowed the NUM president to have accused MacGregor and Thatcher of having been caught lying to miners and public.

Because there was no record of MacGregor's true intentions, Thatcher had no hesitation in authorising an advertising campaign to tell the country that Scargill was lying to his members when he claimed MacGregor planned to 'butcher' the industry by closing 70 pits and shedding 70,000 jobs. She was closely involved in what became a calculated campaign of misinformation as later, at the height of the dispute, she gave her personal approval to a letter in MacGregor's name that was sent to every miner's home. In it the chairman said the NCB was seeking '20,000 voluntary redundancies' and he could state 'categorically and solemnly' that Scargill's claim that 70,000 jobs were at risk was 'absolutely untrue'. The letter was delayed for a week after the Prime Minister asked for a further redrafting and it was finally sent on 21 June 1984, three and a half months into the strike, with a further strengthening of MacGregor's denial: "If these things were true, I would not blame miners for getting angry or for being deeply worried. But these things are absolutely untrue. I state categorically and solemnly. You have been deliberately misled."

Three drafts of the letter are included in the cabinet papers including one with key words heavily underlined. One sentence underscored twice included the line that even if the NUM leadership kept the dispute 'going indefinitely' there could be 'no victory' however long the strike lasted. Continuing the dispute would not result in an 'NUM victory' because 'in the end everyone will lose – and lose disastrously'. If there had ever been any doubt as to her resolve to defeat Scargill, the underlined words served as a reminder that she saw a victory for her government as the only possible outcome. The greater the threat the more determined she became, however deep the unease among cabinet ministers. When the prospect of a potentially disastrous docks strike opened up the possibility of a second front against the government, she rallied Conservative MPs with her infamous pronouncement that she was ready 'to fight the enemy within'.

Her war-like declaration was no slip of the tongue: her cabinet papers disclosed how she had been fired up to mount a 'war of attrition'. She was convinced the task of defeating the 'extreme left' of the trade union movement was as great as that of regaining the Falkland Islands. With military precision she had secretly ordered the build-up of nuclear and oil-fired generation of electricity to ensure indefinite endurance of power supplies and then bought off sympathy strikes, first on the railways, by agreeing to an increase from 4.3 to 4.9 per cent in British Rail's pay offer, and later by a guarantee of employment for 13,000 dockers. Her aim, according to a cabinet office memo, was to 'maintain as far as possible the isolation of the miners from the effective support of the rest of the union movement'.

Mrs Thatcher's conviction that she was in a fight to the finish with the NUM had been strengthened the day before by a private letter of support from the US President Ronald Reagan:

Dear Margaret,

In recent weeks I have thought often of you with considerable empathy as I follow the activities of the miners' and dockworkers' unions... My thoughts are with you... I'm confident as ever that you and your government will come out of this well.

Warm regards. Ron.

Next evening – 19 July 1984 – when addressing a private meeting of Conservative backbenchers, she declared that she had no intention of giving in to the 'industrial muscle' of striking miners who were responsible for 'violence and intimidation like a scar across the face of the country':

We had to fight the enemy without in the Falklands but we must also remember to fight the enemy within.

Her language that evening mirrored the bellicose phraseology of her Downing Street advisers. At cabinet that morning, on being informed of the breakdown in the latest negotiations between the NCB and NUM, she told ministers the government was entering 'a new phase in the dispute' and they had to devise new ways to 'reinforce the pressures on striking miners to return to work'. John Redwood, then head of the Downing Street policy unit and later to become a Conservative minister, had urged her to return to her original strategy of 'encouraging a war of attrition'.

In her memoirs, *The Downing Street Years*, Mrs Thatcher says she was 'enormously relieved' that negotiations with the NUM broke down on 18 July because the failure of talks denied Scargill the chance to 'claim victory'. From then on, her tactic was to get striking miners to realise 'they had no hope of winning and a return to work would begin'. Two of her policy unit's key proposals that July were to play their part as the dispute unfolded. Redwood advised use of the law against secondary picketing and to 'make an attack on the Yorkshire NUM funds'. In the event both strategies were pursued as the strike progressed: working miners went to court to challenge Scargill's repeated declaration that the strike was 'official' and it was their legal action which eventually resulted in the sequestration of the NUM's assets.

From early in the strike, once Thatcher realised the NUM would only accept closure of loss-making pits on condition their coal reserves were exhausted, her advisers urged her time and again to escalate the dispute in order to weaken Scargill's support. Her policy unit's advice was often couched in war-like terminology, and her tactics increasingly reflected the tone, if not always the detail, of secret advice she was given:

Redwood (13 July): You cannot follow a strategy of encouraging a war of attrition ...and a strategy of trying to find a fudged formula...go back to the original strategy of a war of attrition, where the perceived way of the strike ending is for miners to go back to work.

Redwood (29 August): Speedier use of stipendiary magistrates and of legal processes so that pickets can see their comrades being prosecuted and punished quickly for criminal offences...Examining the possibility of mounting a conspiracy charge against union leaders inciting pickets to violence.

Redwood (7 September): The coal industry is comprehensively bust. The activities of the NUM and the attitude of many NCB managers have contrived to ruin a potentially profitable resource industry. Experiments could be made with giving bad mines to miners, along with a substantial capital sum if they were prepared to try and make a go of it themselves... offering the worst mines to miners along with a dowry, would have presentational advantages.

Redwood (21 September): Encourage NCB to extend its threat of dismissal to all those not only convicted of criminal damage against coal board property, but also those convicted of serious offences against persons on picket lines or NCB property.

Redwood (3 October): It is vitally important the NCB should sack any miner convicted of violence against fellow NCB employees or property.

Peter Warry (26 October): We need to regain and retain the initiative...following the NACODS settlement... eliminate the idea that further NCB concessions are just around the corner...place more cards in our hand by upping the stakes...withdraw assurances of no job losses for those that do not return.

Warry (9 November): The screw needs to be gradually tightened...start talking about the possibility of withdrawing capital investment promises in non-working areas.

Warry (13 November): The lengthy strike is causing inexorable geological destruction on faces and whole pits...must at some stage make it impossible for the NCB to continue to guarantee that no striker will ever face compulsory redundancy.

Thatcher's hands-on management of the government's day-to-day response to the dispute by ministers and the NCB was matched by repeated initiatives to curtail the NUM's ability to picket pits where coal production was continuing. Her first behind-the-scenes intervention was at a meeting in Downing Street on 14 March 1984, a mere eight days after the strike started. MacGregor protested about the ease with which 'militants' had succeeded in preventing access for miners who wanted to work. He complained that there had been no arrests. She agreed it was vital to uphold the law to prevent mass picketing. A second meeting was called because it was 'essential to stiffen the resolve of chief constables'. Leon Brittan acknowledged he was not satisfied with the response of chief officers, but he had gone to 'the limit of what the Home Secretary could do while respecting the constitutional independence of police forces'.

Thatcher asked for a fuller report to see if the police were 'adopting the more vigorous interpretation of their duties which was being sought'. Later that day the full cabinet was told that police in Nottinghamshire were 'exercising their powers to stop coaches carrying flying pickets'. But the Prime Minister repeated her demand for more 'vigorous action': the government should provide chief constables with any assistance they needed 'to react with speed and flexibility' before large numbers of pickets were able to assemble.

Her papers confirmed she feared Scargill was about to repeat his 1972 success when flying pickets from Yorkshire succeeded in closing Saltley coke depot, a setback that eventually forced the then Conservative Prime Minister Edward Heath to concede a 27 per cent pay increase for mineworkers. Having become 'deeply disturbed' by the NUM's renewed success in organising flying pickets within a matter of days, she considered it 'vital that criminal law on picketing be upheld'. A note by Thatcher's private secretary Andrew Turnbull set out her absolute determination to thwart Scargill:

> Helping those who volunteered to go to work was not
> sufficient; intimidation had to be ended and people had
> to be free to go about their business without fear. It
> was essential to stiffen the resolve of chief constables to
> ensure that they fulfilled their duty to uphold the law.

Her impatience at the failure to remove the threat of intimidation was even more explicit after a briefing at the second ministerial meeting: 93 pits were open for production at the start of the week, but ten where men were willing to work had since closed due to picketing. A cabinet office memo left no doubt as to Thatcher's frustration: "It was essential for the government to be seen to be upholding the criminal law on picketing...It appeared that the police were not carrying out their duties fully as large pickets were being permitted and few arrests were being made." Within four days of her intervention police started to turn back flying pickets from Yorkshire who were heading south on the motorway to Midlands and Nottinghamshire coalfields. Striking miners from Kent were being turned back at the Dartford Tunnel. In news reports next day, the chief constable of Humberside, who was co-ordinating the operation, denied police had become the Conservative Party's political weapon. Their job was to ensure 'the rule of law' was maintained.

De-classified reports presented at cabinet and weekly ministerial meetings indicated the degree of control being exercised by the Prime Minister. She had demanded regular, updated information on police activity, including latest figures for arrests and court cases. By the second week of the strike, the Home Secretary was reporting that a total of 7,245 police officers were on duty in Nottinghamshire to protect miners reporting for work. One option considered was the use of military helicopters to take even more police officers to working coalfields. Thatcher told the Home Office to respond in 'a sympathetic and generous way' towards the additional cost of providing police support for Nottinghamshire. As the number of arrests increased, she began to congratulate police on their efforts. A month into the strike, after more than 100 arrests at Creswell colliery in Derbyshire, which had been besieged by 1,000 pickets, she said it was 'totally wrong and false' for the NUM to accuse police of being heavy handed; it was a slur on the police for the 'superb way they have kept open a man's right to go to his place of work unmolested'.

To counter the spread of mass picketing, Thatcher ordered a full review of police tactics and criminal law enforcement. In June 1984 the Attorney General, Sir Michael Havers, assured her that criminal law was sufficient 'to embrace all the mischiefs' which had manifested themselves. Despite mounting criticism of the practice of turning back pickets on main roads and motorways, law officers were confident about the effectiveness of 'well-established principles of common law' regarding police powers to stop people travelling to the scene of an actual or apprehended breach of the peace. He thought the police had achieved 'a greater degree of success' than in any similar law-and-order confrontation. A key factor had been the 'deployment of thousands of additional police officers in the areas concerned'; chief constables had not lacked the manpower they thought necessary. But eight months into the strike, a secret Home Office report admitted the interception of pickets could have been counterproductive. Stopping them at police boundaries and turning them back from likely sites of trouble might merely have diverted them to other destinations. The problem was that once diverted there was 'no longer such good information' about where they were likely to go.

Thatcher's impatience at slow progress in the courts prompted further secret initiatives to counter the public's impression that the union was escaping justice in extending the strike. As arrests mounted for breaches of the peace, obstruction and criminal damage, so did her intolerance at the lack of prosecutions. By 16 July 1984 magistrates had dealt with only 20 per cent of 2,800 cases which were pending. Two top government law officers, Havers and Lord Chancellor, Lord Hailsham, had both been under pressure for some weeks to do more to exercise their authority after Thatcher discovered that magistrates in Rotherham and

Mansfield were 'dragging their feet' in dealing with cases involving pickets arrested for pit-head violence.

She demanded action to speed up the process because failure to deal with indictable offences was giving the impression that 'Scargill and his union were above the law'. But Hailsham clearly had concerns about applying pressure on police and courts. In May 1984, after over 900 arrests in the Nottinghamshire coalfield, he told Thatcher that the chief constable of Nottinghamshire had 'expressed reservations about the quality of some of the evidence upon which the arrests have been made, and for this reason is not anxious for dates of trial to be fixed too soon'. Downing Street must have challenged Hailsham because he re-worded his letter to say the chief constable was 'anxious lest the delay causes the quality of the evidence available to deteriorate'.

Havers had recommended that Hailsham should 'remind, if necessary, enforce' the magistrates' courts to accept stipendiary magistrates, and later he was able to reassure Thatcher that steps had been taken. "Today the ring round of the clerks to the justices has started...the un-co-operative courts have now been warned that a stipendiary will be appointed if the backlog justifies, whether they request it or not."

Nonetheless Hailsham's disclosure that Nottinghamshire's chief constable was worried about the 'quality of the evidence' was a significant revelation given the post-strike demands for an investigation into the conduct of South Yorkshire police which arrested 95 pickets for riot and unlawful assembly during the 'Battle of Orgreave'. All were acquitted after defence lawyers argued that police evidence had been fabricated.

Among the de-classified documents were notes and letters which confirmed suspicions that Thatcher and her cabinet had forged a close working relationship with the

South Yorkshire force. Four months into the strike, the chief constable, the late Peter Wright, was given secret authorisation to go on incurring the additional cost of bringing in police reinforcements to help ensure the resumption of deliveries from British Steel Corporation's coking plant at Orgreave. In the corner of one document was her hand-written note asking: "Can we provide the funds direct?"

Wright's tactics in commanding the massive police operation required to control mass picketing at Orgreave had already been condemned by South Yorkshire County Council and its Labour majority on the South Yorkshire Police Authority, which both supported the NUM. After the county council passed a resolution calling for Orgreave to be closed, the police authority withdrew Wright's discretion to spend up to £2,000 without prior authority. Brittan and Havers took swift action on 3 July to support Wright, and set in train a series of secret contingency measures. Confidential correspondence revealed that the Home Secretary proposed that the Treasury Solicitor should immediately make funds available if required by the chief constable.

Wright intended to prepare a local RAF barracks to accommodate police support units needed to reinforce South Yorkshire police, ready for the re-opening of Orgreave the following Monday. Brittan advised Thatcher: "We need to move quickly in this way to forestall public speculation that police operations against the dispute will be hampered, or even that the armed forces would have to be brought in instead." Next day, at a ministerial meeting in Downing Street, Havers said he was seeking a judicial review of the police authority's decision. He was also considering whether to seek an injunction to prevent the authority from suspending its chief constable on 'improper grounds'. At cabinet, Brittan reported that police operations to control picketing in South Yorkshire had continued to be successful and the following day the authority was ordered to suspend its action against the chief constable pending a further court hearing.

Brittan feared that other police authorities under political control sympathetic to the miners' strike might copy South Yorkshire's tactic. The previous month the Merseyside Police Authority had attempted to prevent its chief constable from sending reinforcements to help prevent mass picketing. In backing steps taken by her Home Secretary and Attorney General, Thatcher said the South Yorkshire chief constable should be given 'every support'. It was most important that police authorities should not be allowed to 'interfere with the operational judgement of chief constables in policing the dispute'. Wright was supported again by Brittan in September after his 'left-wing' police authority said it intended to 'phase out all horses and some dogs' from the South Yorkshire force, a proposal which Brittan said would result in the authority failing to carry out its statutory responsibilities to maintain 'an efficient police force'. After an escalation that same month in picket-line violence outside the Maltby pit, Wright assured Brittan that his force required 'no additional resources'.

What the documents revealed was the extent of a remarkably effective relationship between the government of the day and an individual police force, almost as if there was a hot-line between a chief constable and the cabinet, even perhaps the Prime Minister. The closeness of that co-operation must have had an impact on the working practices of Wright and his fellow officers and cannot be ignored given the subsequent, disastrous response of the South Yorkshire force at the 1989 Hillsborough stadium disaster. Did the unprecedented ministerial support five years earlier for their handling of the 'Battle of Orgreave' create a sense of security, a mindset that meant that whatever happened officers felt safe in the knowledge they would get government

support? Thatcher's 1984 papers have helped to prise open a window on events that the Orgreave Truth and Justice Campaign has worked tirelessly to expose. Journalists can offer only a resumé of what is contained in the vast bundles of government papers de-classified each year, a first draft of what we hope future historians will return to with a far harsher spotlight.

Who We Are: the Photographs of Martin Jenkinson
Granville Williams

George "Geordie" Brealey, the miner featured in Martin Jenkinson's photograph at Orgreave during the 1984-85 miners' strike, is engaged in humorous banter with a policeman as he 'inspects' the police lines wearing his toy policeman's helmet.

There's another photograph, by *The Guardian*'s Don McPhee, where the two face each other with fixed expressions. Both pictures have been widely reproduced since – in books, magazines, on T-shirts – but it is the Jenkinson photograph that does it for me. It is one of a number of powerful photographs Martin took during the epic year-long strike when he was the official photographer working for the Yorkshire Area NUM and their paper *The Yorkshire Miner*.

Martin Jenkinson died from cancer in February 2012. The former 'steel city', Sheffield in South Yorkshire, has now honoured him with an exhibition *Who We Are* containing over 80 of his photographs. The exhibition, in a generously large space at Weston Park Museum, did him proud.

You were immediately drawn into the breadth of his work by a wall display of all his press passes for the events he covered, from a UB40 gig to the People's March for Jobs, from trade union conferences to the pit camps set up in the wake of the Tory government's plan announced in October 1993 to close 31 pits with the loss of 31,000 jobs.

There was also a life-size mock-up of Martin's 'studio' – in reality it was in a gloomy garage. Mark Harvey, a photographer friend of Martin's, spoke on the opening night of the Weston Park exhibition and acknowledged it was the first time he had seen it so clearly. He pointed out one exhibit from the office – a bulky Canon digital camera, one of the first to be made, which Martin used.

Martin moved to Sheffield with his wife Edwina and daughter Justine in 1976. For three years he worked in the steel industry. After being made redundant in 1979 he found a job on a local community newspaper, *The Woodpecker*, using his hobby – photography – to earn a living.

I grew up in Sheffield in the 1950s when it was an economically vibrant city with an unrivalled public transport system with low fares which enabled people to get around the city quickly and cheaply. Martin's photography bears witness to a different city, one bearing the brunt of the ravages of Thatcherism, the attacks on jobs and living standards, and the surge in unemployment.

Martin's strong sense of social justice, fairness and equality shines through all his work – exemplified in the photograph of a striking miner in South Yorkshire digging through the snow to find coal to heat his home.

But the exhibition also reflects another important aspect to his work – the images of the pathos and humour of everyday working-class life in and around Sheffield: among them Von, a newspaper vendor; Maxine Duffus, Sheffield's first black female bus driver, and the 1,500 unemployed people queuing to apply for 50 jobs at a restaurant in Sheffield in 1983.

● *Who We Are: Photographs of Martin Jenkinson was at Weston Park Museum from 24 November 2018 -14 April 2019.*

Top: 1500 queue for 50 jobs, bottom: Maxine Duffus

137

Miner digging for coal, Thurnscoe, South Yorkshire

Top: George 'Geordie' Brealey at Orgreave 1984, bottom: WAPC pit camp, Armthorpe, South Yorkshire

Shafton NUM banner, Durham Gala 1993

Out of the ashes: The Durham Miners' Gala
Huw Beynon

Introduction

In 2018 Amber A' Lee Frost, a political activist from New York, wrote a 'dispatch from the North of England' in her blog. It focused on the miners' strike and 'historical memory' and began in this way:

> I was sitting in the Pitman's Parliament or Council Chamber, at Redhills – the somewhat faded yet still undeniably grand and stately union hall that has remained headquarters for the Durham Miners' Association since its construction in 1915 when the union's membership was swelling past 150,000 and they required a new, larger building.
>
> The last pit in the Durham coalfield closed in 1993 but I was nonetheless there to attend the 134th Durham Miners' Gala – still the largest trade union event of its kind, with around a hundred thousand attendees, all there to celebrate the power of the labor movement and the men of a once-massive industrial labor union that essentially no longer exists. Everyone I met radiated a resilient hope and joy. It was pleasantly confounding.[1]

Here, she presents us with a puzzle: how is it possible for a union that no longer exists to operate not in a depressed state and on a shoestring but through determinedly retaining its large and grand premises of yesteryear, still successfully organising an annual, celebratory event prominent in the international calendar of labour supporters? Why too, given the scale of the collapse of the coal industry and the persistent removal of the architecture of the industry changing the landscape, can the people of the area still look to the past for a sense of purpose not with despair but with 'resilient joy and hope'.

The Big Meeting

One part of the answer was provided by *The Guardian* which, on 12 July 2013, ran an editorial under the heading 'In Praise of the Durham Miners' Gala'. 'Tomorrow,' it read:

...Durham's narrow streets will be thronged with thousands of people, young and old, from the county's pit villages. .... Don't ever say 'former' pit villages, even if the last mine closed in 1993. The colliery banners and bands processing for hours through the city will tell us otherwise. .... Once, all aspiring Labour politicians needed to be seen there. It remains a politically and emotionally charged day for the working people of Durham. Nostalgia? Not when you see the bonds of connection and common purpose that such communities in the North East feel.

Here no mention is made of 1984 when those same communities, sharing a common purpose for strike action in the Durham Area, joined others in a concerted attempt to prevent the hastening closure of the mines and the destruction of the industry. The absence is not surprising, the newspaper had been more lukewarm in its support at that time – but it is an important omission, for the experience of the strike had a lasting effect. David Temple reflected in 2014:

Yes 30 years on. I often think how poorer our lives would have been without that year. If we had just faded away without a fight I am sure there would now be no Gala to boost our sense of wellbeing each year. But more importantly it has become a symbol of resistance and a rallying point which is quite extraordinary. The whole question of the state is looked on differently now.

In the late seventies, in spite of the militancy shown in the two successful national strikes, there had been a great sense of things fading away in Durham. Coal mines closed at regular intervals and this accelerated in the eighties as coking coal was imported into the steel complex at Redcar. The Gala changed too, becoming smaller year after year, supplemented one year by marching 'jazz bands' of school girls playing kazoos led by drum majorettes. At that time, Tom Callan the regional secretary of the NUM had accepted that the Gala would dwindle and eventually finish. For him the only hope was that it could be boosted, in the short term, through its contribution to the tourist industry. There was deep resistance to turning it into a 'political' event or to one that involved other trade unions.

At that time Dave Ayre was secretary of the Wear Valley Trades Council. A bricklayer by trade, he had a deep affection for the Gala and remembered that his father, a miner, 'used to carry me on his shoulders to the Big Meeting in Durham when I was a baby'. In 1979 he had become concerned for the future of the Gala feeling that:

.... although it's developed into more of a carnival now it could still be a good political demonstration .... through the trades council we have tried to move it in that direction but the NUM have never accepted it. We wanted to expand it by including other trade unions and trades council, because there aren't many miners' lodges left now, except round the coast. But the NUM won't have any other union representation; they want it kept as a miners' gala. (Ayre, 1979:8)

In this way, therefore, the past was inherited as ritual. Things were done as they were always done because they were always done that way. There was an example of this in 1981 when the Durham Area participated in the TUC's march against unemployment in Liverpool. One of the delegation, Jim Ellison, began to chant: "Maggie, Maggie Maggie...Out. Out Out!" For this he was reprimanded by the Area Secretary and told: "The Durham miners always march in silence."

But things were to change. The overwhelming victory

by Arthur Scargill in the election for the Presidency of the NUM was followed by the appointment of MacGregor as Chair of the NCB and these were seen as decisive factors and a portend of conflict and struggle. By coincidence 1983 also marked the centenary of the Gala. The first of these 'Big Meetings' had taken place in 1871, two years after the formation of the Durham Miners' Association. Then it had been held at Wharton Park on the edge of the city but later and in subsequent years it took place on the racecourse ground in the city centre on the second Saturday in July: an event interrupted only by war and strike.

In the commemoration of this important event it was decided to break with tradition and, in the areas where the mines had closed, encourage the villagers to join the parade, marching, wherever possible, behind their old banners. Lodges and officials from other areas of the NUM were also invited to attend, and the Tower Lodge from Hirwain in South Wales made the long journey north. Earlier in the year, while on strike, the Tower men had visited Durham seeking support for their attempt to halt pit closures. Subsequently they had 'twinned' with Easington Colliery and were determined to attend the Gala in July. On that day Arthur Scargill and Neil Kinnock (who was standing for the leadership of the Labour Party) were the main speakers, both emphasising the deep significance of coal mining communities with Scargill reiterating his prediction of a 'hit list': pits in Durham were going to close, mining villages and communities would be destroyed.

The Durham Miners' Association (DMA) commissioned a video to be made of the day and in capturing the event it gave a clear visual demonstration of what had been lost. Viewed today *The Big Meeting* conveys the complex mixture of feeling that contributed to the occasion when the people of all the mining villages came together. In Easington the band walked through the village and played outside the houses of the retired miners, reviving memories of the disaster that took place in the pit in 1951. Then onto the buses to Durham to march together through the city behind their local lodge banner as the music played by the colliery bands filled the streets. Marching on to the Racecourse to listen to the speeches while first standing in silence as a band played *Gresford* – the Miners' Hymn – written by Durham miner Robert Saint after the dreadful event that had taken 266 lives in the North Wales colliery in 1934 – the last of the disasters under private enterprise.[2]

People said that on that day, it was as things used to be. A turning back of the clock. Michael Foot spoke there in 1947 and when I interviewed him in 1981 he remembered that:

> …in those days it was absolutely sensational. There were so many lodges you see and they had to start bringing them in at half past eight in the morning.[3] The whole city absolutely throbbed with the thing from early in the morning right through until you left. And you left absolutely drunk with it – the music, the banners and all in that beautiful city. It overwhelmed you really. In those days it was, far and away, the best working class festival that there was in this country. Far and away the best. It was just marvellous.

For the local people it had a deeper meaning. As one ex-miner from the East Hetton colliery in Kelloe explained:

> It stirred the insides of your soul and you didn't know whether to laugh or burst out crying all day. It's part of our heritage that; part of the working class; part of our lives. It was something we always treasured.[4]

But in 1983 the feelings for the past were mixed with worries and some fears about the future. The video carries a deep sense of what was to come. One year later and the coalfield was on strike and the Gala cancelled. This was an established practice, although in 1926 a small unofficial gala took place in the village of Burnhope away from the

145

citadel of Durham. In 1984, however, things changed and it was decided that all areas of the NUM and all trade unions should be invited to take part in a demonstration in support of the strike. This was achieved through a radical change in the composition and tenure of the executive committee, something brought about by rank and file organisation across the east coast lodges. The demonstration was a tremendous success and deeply emphasised the power of the occasion and the extent of trade union solidarity.

In the aftermath of the strike Dave Hopper and Dave Guy filled the vacant posts for the Durham Miners and joined Bill Etherington of the Durham Mechanics in the new left wing area leadership, clear that the demonstration of 1984 showed the way forward for the Big Meeting. Pits closed, but the lodges of Herrington, Horden and Sacriston were encouraged to be involved as were others like Bearpark and East Hetton that had closed before the strike. Other trade unions were encouraged to participate. It was a major change.

From industry to community organising
But in the early nineties everything changed. In spite of a re-energised national campaign to save coal mining, the coastal collieries were closed. In the first edition of *Shafted* I wrote of these events and how an area that for two centuries had been built around an economy based on a coal mining industry was left bereft.[5] The miners' union was also left short of funds and without an income from its members' dues. As George Robson, the union's former Finance Officer, recalled, the strike and the campaigning had weakened the union's reserves:

> Before that we were well off with 50 per cent of our income from NUM members' contributions and 50 per cent from investments with merchant banks in London. But after the strike and the Campaign For Coal to try to

save the pits we were ruined (Robson, 2010:66)

This raised questions about the future viability of the union and the Big Meeting. For some, the ending of the industry took away the very purpose of the trade union and with it the annual gala. Mick Carr, a member of the Durham Colliery Mechanics Association (DCMA), who had worked at the Horden and Wearmouth collieries, felt that the gala should end. In his view it would be wrong for it to continue as it would lack the necessary authenticity. He worried that it would fizzle out, or be kept going to feed the egos of a few. 'No Miners – No Gala' was the slogan of a group that would meet together at the Colpitts pub in Durham on Gala Day in protest. However theirs was a minority view and as Mick Carr's friend David Temple was to point out:

> On July 10 1993, the local mining communities poured onto the streets of Durham in greater numbers than had been seen for twenty years. Again many old banners, frail and faded from the winds of past galas, were lifted from their resting places and brought out into the streets ...The message was unmistakable – this is our Gala; it expresses who we are; it must go on. (Temple, 2012:168)

This proved to be convincing evidence of the possibility of the Gala being authentically reconfigured as a permanent event, outlasting the mines but building on the culture and politics of mining. It was in this spirit that Dave Hopper, in his vote of thanks closing the day, announced, to loud applause, "We will be back next year spearheading a campaign for all workers in struggle."

Once committed to this future, the area leadership and executive committee faced the problem of replacing their depleted reserves with a new source of income that would allow the Gala to continue, and the trade union to remain as a viable organisation most especially in relation to fighting compensation claims. They received some early help from

Michael Watt a New Zealand business man who, before making his fortune, had worked alongside ex-Durham miners in the 1980s. He had enjoyed their company and had been moved by their talk of the strike and also of Big Meeting days in Durham. All of which made him amendable to providing a grant to the union to cover the costs of the Gala through until 1999.

The final closure of all mining of course meant that the National Union of Miners could no longer be recognised by the Registrar of Friendly Societies as a trade union in the North East. It was in this context that the DMA and the DCMA were re-established as organisations set up to support and seek compensation and legal redress for their members. An Affiliated Membership Scheme was set up with an annual fee of £20 to ex-miners. This would allow the union to continue to support members in employment and medical tribunals and to take forward the compensation work that was to become a critical aspect of its activities. It was agreed that small deductions (7% capped at £1,000) would be made from successful claims.

The fight for the compensation of ex-miners was assisted by the close links that the new DMA leadership had built with the Thompson firm of labour lawyers during the strike. Pickets who had been arrested and locked up began demanding better legal support, and Geoff Shears, the head of the Thompson's office in Newcastle, together with Tony Briscoe and Mark Berry became actively involved in speaking at a weekend NUM school in Durham in September 1984.[6]

Subsequently Thompsons represented the miners and were particularly supportive in relation to injury compensation. With this legal support Dave Hopper and Dave Guy were determined to take the risk of pursuing a long-held grievance against the coal employer for damages due to its negligence in relation to both bronchitis and chronic emphysema and also vibration white finger. In doing so they knew that the costs of losing would be catastrophic but it was felt that the case was both strong and just. It was a continuation of the struggle and it turned out to be hugely successful on both counts, obtaining significant funds in compensation for its retired members and also highlighting the conditions under which miners had worked in the nationalised industry. Some of the judicial decisions contained the harshest words ever spoken about the National Coal Board's lack of care in the treatment of its employees.

By 2008 Shears had become Chief Executive of Thompson and, speaking at the Gala, he paid tribute to the work of the DMA compensation department when he said:

Vibration white finger, chronic bronchitis and emphysema cases arose at that time when the Union was on its knees and there was a massive financial risk in fighting test cases and the government refused to meet its responsibilities to negotiate a compensation scheme. The DMA backed test cases and risked everything it had so that its solicitors could prove British Coal was to blame for the miners' injuries and diseases over decades. As a result, the Government's own figures prove that Durham Miners and Mechanics have the highest success rate and the highest level of compensation in the country – a success that has helped all workers. Many have supported the Union financially and as a result the DMA has consolidated and will expand its services. It has sustained and is developing the infrastructure of the lodges which keep people together and because of that the Gala will continue.

The pursuit of compensation from the NCB had given a new purpose to the organisation as did the continuing need of ex-miners and their families for support and advice in the face of cuts in welfare provision. In this way the industrial union became a community union fighting and dealing with the state. As a consequence some remnants of the lodge structure of the union remained in many of the villages where mines had closed. In the most recent closures, like those on the coast, lodge officials remained in post. Men like Irving Lyons in Horden and Alan Johnson in Dawdon remained active as a source of social support, legal advice, leadership and organisation. At Easington Colliery an active lodge remained in place with Alan Cummings as secretary for decades after the mine had closed. Like Lyons and Johnson he also sat on the executive committee of the DMA and was active in defending members in employment and medical tribunals. These men, like the area leadership, were determined to continue supporting the Gala and encouraged the other ex-mining villages to follow, reviving their old banners and marching in Durham City. Reflecting on this in 1999, Alan Cummings found it uplifting that: "It's all organised by ordinary people, not people with degrees or lots of education, just ordinary practical working class people who know what to do and get things done."

Banners and people

The decision by the DMA to continue with the Gala and to offer an open invitation to all of the closed lodges to participate had a profound impact producing a cumulative process of change. Historically, the lodge had been an expression of both the mine and the community around it and this was symbolised in the lodge banner. I once asked a group of Durham miners whether it was possible to have a lodge without a banner. My question was ridiculed: you could not have a lodge without a banner. It had been that way from the very beginning. At the first Gala in 1871 the *Sunderland Times* reported that:

> Each of the lodges and its accompanying friends
> marched in procession through the town from the
> railway stations .... to the meeting place, and a great

feature was the banners that they carried. (20 July, 1871)

In the following year the *Durham Chronicle* made clear that:
The display of banners was a prominent and pleasing feature of the demonstration. Altogether there were upward of 70 flags on the ground. They were arranged around the full length of the field… The greater proportion of them were indeed artistic productions both in design and execution. (18 July 1872)

The banner as both work of art and the symbolic representation of the people of the lodge has been an enduring feature of Durham life. The re-establishment of the Gala ignited quests across the county to search for the old banners. Some of these, like at Chopwell, were on display in local community centres; others, like the one at Dean and Chapter, had fallen into complete disrepair. In these cases, 'banner groups' and 'banner partnerships' began to be established across the coalfield in a spontaneous movement that mirrored the developments of the support groups during the 1984-85 miners' strike. They met and did research into the local banner, some thought of a new banner with new designs, others wanted to produce a complete replica of the original banner seen in photographs. Encouraged and supported by the DMA these groups met with the aim of accumulating funds locally (through raffles and other events) and applying for aid from the Heritage Lottery Fund to meet the costs of repair and production of banners. At the time the fund was being criticised for the lack of support it had given to poorer areas, and particularly the old coalfields. Its claim that this was a consequence of the low number of applications, was further encouragement to the emerging banner groups and this fortunate coincidence led to many successful applications from Durham. In 2001, the New Herrington banner partnership had been the first to successfully obtain funding and commission a replica banner. The lodge secretary was centrally involved and he made it clear that:

Part of what we do is about letting Thatcher and her like know we are still here. They closed the pits and took the jobs, but every time we take that Banner out, we are saying to them: "We're still here, and we are still fighting for our communities." (quoted in Stephenson and Wray, 2005)

In this way, and with the support and involvement of the DMA, the villagers commissioned facsimiles of old banners or planned new designs for banners that would link them with the past age of mining. These banners provided a new focus for village life that built organically on the past, making clear the symbolic power of the image, portrayed in silk and carried through the streets of the city.

The DMA played an important part in all this. Under the new leadership, the officials and executive members regularly attended meetings and offered advice and coordinated the involvement of new banners in the annual parade. Each year that followed the strike new banners appeared from the lodges of mines long closed, and their re-appearance pointed to a new development in the organisation of solidarity. On many occasions they linked up with local community workers funded by the local authority or by one of many charitable funders and organisations. These workers were most often women and concerned with dealing with issues of community development and the problems of dislocation and lack of employment in the area. The banner groups provided a focus for their activities while also linking them with the lodges and the organisation of the old trade union, providing advice on funding applications, adding a new level of expertise, helping the communities to help themselves. The groups also provided a focus for other activities (local history, photography) with a capacity to engage with people of all ages. These developments in Durham, built around the banner and the Big Meeting, revealed the capacity of deindustrialised communities and a (defunct) trade union to build on the past and build bridges across a segregated working class. These developments were strengthened in 2008 when the local community-led banner groups were coordinated across the region through the Durham Mining Communities Banner Group Association.

A change of politics
In the Gala's heydays in the years after the war the guest of honour at the Big Meeting had been the leader of the Labour Party accompanied by other guests chosen from within the Labour elite and sympathetic international dignitaries. Under the leadership of Sam Watson it had been carefully crafted so that Durham in July became an important date in the Labour calendar and one where, through informal conversation at dinner on the Friday night, important discussion took place and agreements made. Watson realised the importance of the setting and he used it diligently in orchestrating support for his right of centre politics. These arrangements outlived him and continued with the support of the NCB. Here again the strike changed everything.

Neil Kinnock spoke in 1985, but the muted reception to his speech and the obvious antagonism felt toward him by many following his interventions during the strike led him to refuse further invitations. This pattern of refusal continued under the leadership of Smith, Blair and Brown. In contrast, guests and speakers began to be drawn from beyond the political elite and with internationalism of a different kind, with speakers from, for example, Cuba and Chile. So dramatic was this change that at the Gala of 2013, in the middle of a major economic crisis, no Labour MP or Lord spoke from the platform. Not since the days of Keir Hardie had this happened, and it seemed like a significant moment. The speakers included the General Secretary of the

TUC, trade union general secretaries, left wing journalists and representatives of the Hillsborough families and the Shrewsbury Pickets. For a moment it seemed that we were seeing in embryo the new kind of labour movement made up of trade unions, social movements and single issue campaigners, capable of engaging civil society, and challenging the power of the new political elites and their orthodoxy of neo-liberalism.

This change in the platform of speakers at the Gala paralleled the way in which the DMA had come to relate to the broader trade union movement. A close relationship had developed with the TGWU at the end of the eighties when it seemed possible that the NUM might merge with the large general union. In the preliminary discussions Dave Hopper and Dave Guy met with like-minded officials in the TGWU, one of whom was ex-car worker Eddie Roberts. He was invited to the Gala in 1990 and was incredibly moved by the experience. In his view:

> Anyone who fails to be impressed and enthused by
> the atmosphere of the Big Meeting is not human and
> certainly not part of our Movement. We had little
> inkling of the size, but what mostly impressed me was
> the fact that although there were so few working pits the
> turnout was enormous. It defied description and has to
> be experienced in the flesh. It was extremely exhilarating
> and to us it became our annual pilgrimage.

He encouraged others to attend, including Tony Woodley who was moved by the occasion and particularly impressed by the kinds of discussions that he engaged with at the eve of gala dinner. He encouraged workers from the Vauxhall plant in Ellesmere Port to attend and, when made General Secretary, fully endorsed links between the union and the Gala, links that were later maintained by Len McCluskey. At that time with trade union membership in decline, McCluskey, like other national trade union leaders, was receptive to developing links with social movements and of the importance of popular campaigning as a way of widening their support. The re-emergence at Durham of the Gala as a platform for left-wing ideas and discussion was therefore both timely and welcomed. Many trade unionists travelled north (and south) for the event and, speaking with them, they often mentioned having their 'batteries recharged' and of experiencing 'something unique'. It was an enormously successful collaboration that saw the Gala transformed from a small local meeting of coal miners into a broadly based national trade union and working class celebration. In speaking of its impact Roberts pointed to the way that attending the Gala provided visitors with a sense of hope, a break from the feeling of isolation and being alone: "You realise that there are so many people out there who do actually think along the same lines as you. This is a very important role that the Gala plays, whether consciously or otherwise."

Marras

These different changes, moving along in parallel, saw the DMA and its annual Gala continuing into the twenty first century. In this it had managed to transform the event both locally and nationally with more and more villages being involved and drawing upon the support of many national unions. However there remained the worry about the sustainability of both the Gala and the union. Finance was a persistent concern as was the passage of time and with it the ageing of the area and lodge leadership. The DMA President David Guy, after several years of serious illness, died in 2012 and this focussed attention upon the long term future of both organisations. This was sharpened in 2016 when David Hopper died suddenly. Hopper's funeral was held at the miners' hall Redhills. It was attended by well over 500 people with officials for all the main national trade unions represented (*Durham Miner*, 17, 2016; Beynon,

2017). Just a month earlier they had all attended the Gala in Durham that was deemed to have been 'the greatest ever'. At that time it seemed that the significance of the annual event and its national importance had been finally sealed. At the funeral however there were many questioning thoughts about the future.

Dave Hopper had often commented (sometimes with surprise) on the ways in which the miners were regarded and treated by the other trade unions. He felt that as an official of the DMA he was cut a lot of slack. This was especially true after the demonstration in 1992 and the final closures of the area's mines. The fact that the miners had struggled to prevent closures and the fact that the closures had happened as predicted led many to agree that 'Scargill was right'. Perhaps in the goodwill afforded to the miners in the North East guilt was mixed with admiration. Whatever the reason, this support and solidarity could be used to strengthen and support the Gala if the right mechanism could be found. This appeared in the form of the Friends of the Durham Miners' Gala (FODMG), the brainchild of David Temple.

David Temple had been a mechanic at the Murton colliery and during the strike had sat on the executive committee of the DCMA. As a one time member of the Workers' Revolutionary Party he had written and sold pamphlets about the history of mining and had a keen interest in printing and publishing. This was realised in 1986 when, through the aid of a bank loan, he purchased premises in Newcastle that would house the Trade Union Printing Services (TUPS), giving employment to young men and to a close friend who had been sacked at the Tursdale workshops during the strike. Under the new leadership of the DMA, TUPS came to produce the annual Gala brochure. Keith Pattison, who had taken memorable photographs at Easington during the strike, also became involved making videos of the gala and also of the annual event that was organised to celebrate the life of the eighteenth century trade unionist Thomas Hebburn. Ross Forbes was also drawn in. During the strike the NUJ had decided that the Durham Area needed support with its media relations and Forbes had been appointed as press secretary. He stayed on until the pits closed down and he still remembered that experience vividly, recalling how 'relationships you made in the maelstrom of 1985 were always a benchmark for future life. Those were some of the best people you could ever want to meet'. Thompson's Solicitors through Mark Berry and later Ian McFaul were also involved with advice and conversation. Many more too.

Once set up the FODMG became an active web-based support group that asks for subscription to help the Gala from Friends. These friends are termed 'marras'. In the early form of coal mining in Durham the work was done by pairs of miners who were usually friends and called each other 'marras'. Such was the strength and ubiquity of mining that the work term became a general term for a friend. As such the membership card of the FODMG notes:

Marra: (noun)
Miners' term of affection for a trusted friend. Marras were generally workmates to whom, quite often, you entrusted your life. Marras are comrades who stick together.

In this way, and quite brilliantly, the old culture of the mines was transposed into the contemporary context, adding more meaning to the act of giving financial support. And the financial support was significant – life-saving in fact. In his address at the eve of Gala dinner in 2017, the new secretary of the DMA, Alan Cummings, was fulsome in his thanks to Temple and the organisation for the financial assistance it had provided for the event.

The big problem – as with all affairs of trade unions –

related to the constitution of the new organisation with the need to carefully navigate the choppy waters between it and the DMA. It was agreed that its Governing Board would be made up of the fourteen northern trade unions including the DMA, with a Board of Directors elected from its number. Grahame Morris MP for Easington filled the role of Chairman. [7] Given the need for openness and transparency, Thompson's advised that the organisation should be registered as a not-for-profit company and this was finally agreed in 2016. Through this scheme, subscriptions were made by three categories of member: national union, trade union branches and individuals. This scheme attracted notable individuals like the Tyneside actor Alun Armstrong and it grew in popularity, encouraging optimism about the Gala as being both sustainable and re-energised as a popular political and cultural event in North. Some talked of it as a working class Glastonbury.

Cultural renaissance

These changes in the Big Meeting were mirrored in the transformation in the Redhills Miners' Hall. Since the strike and under the new leadership this had been changed beyond recognition. It had once been an austere place, the centre of the trade union and the place where rules were made and enforced. Dave Hopper remembered, as a young miner, approaching the building with a mixture of 'fear and awe'. After the closures of the sixties and through the seventies it, like the industry itself, had gone through decline. Visiting it, you were impressed by the architecture, the statues of the old leaders that stood on plinths along the driveway, and by the silence that invoked a sense of reverence, but also registered an emptiness. Barry Chambers remembered an occasion when, in 1981, as secretary of the Blackhall Lodge, he was involved in a fierce discussion on the ground floor of the building when Harold Mitchell the President came to the top of the stairs telling them to be quiet because 'this is not a miners' hall'. Barry felt that this said it all because 'that is just what it is. It is a bloody miners' hall'.

Here again the strike changed everything. It was the centre of everything during those twelve months and under the new leadership it retained this openness and became a much more lively and inviting place, often carrying banners in support of local and national campaigns. It became a centre for film – *The Happy Lands* and *Still the Enemy Within* were both screened there to large audiences – and for exhibitions and discussions of mining history and culture. However it was extremely expensive to heat and to maintain and this emerged as a major issue.

In 2016 when Alan Cummings took over as general secretary with Joe Whitworth (also of the Easington Lodge) as chairman, he was overwhelmed by the scale of the financial crisis facing the DMA. In 2012 it had extended its pursuit of compensation for industrial injury by pursuing cases of osteoarthritis of the knee. This failed in the High Court, leaving the DMA liable for up to £2 million in costs. In spite of this the DMA had continued with its support for ex-miners on sickness benefit and undergoing 'work-capability assessments' as part of the government's austerity programme. It had also retained its leading role in the battle for industrial injury. The casework collected in Durham played an important part in influencing the recommendation made by the Industrial Injury Advisory Council to have Dupuytren's Contracture – the distorting injury to the fingers, brought about by the excessive use of vibratory tools – registered as an industrial disease. It took the government four and a half years to act, as Alan Cummings explained:

It is a disgrace that it has taken so long, and that
there has been such resistance from this Government.
Dupuytren's Contracture is a serious and debilitating

159

condition for many people, affecting their ability to carry out day-to-day tasks .... We are glad that those suffering will begin to receive help – it will make a real difference to their lives.

However the financial problems persisted and were only eased temporarily by the conversion of the old miners' agents' houses into student accommodation and then by a generous loan from the Yorkshire Area of the NUM. Mining had continued in Yorkshire and only ended with the closure of the last UK colliery at Kellingley in 2015, 23 years after mining ended in Durham. Given this breathing space, thought turned to the Heritage Lottery Fund as a possible source of funds to permanently secure the future of the building. In order to develop a bid, the DMA obtained a grant from the Coal Industry Social Welfare Organisation (CISWO). This was used to fund the appointment of Ross Forbes whose new responsibilities included the organisation of the Gala. However the main focus was to be on Redhills. Alan Cummings explained in 2018 that:

The intention is to leave a vibrant and active legacy to the county which keeps our value and traditions alive. We are looking towards Redhills future as much as its past.

At that time *Historic England* had put out a call for places in the country that were irreplaceable and in need of restoration and support. The Council Chamber at Redhills, once known as the Pitman's Parliament, was seen to be a possible entrant. After some research, a bid was put together and to much amazement was successful. The Pitman's Parliament hall was judged to be one of the top hundred irreplaceable places in Britain, standing alongside Westminster as the only debating chamber. This success was hugely significant, increasing the confidence that people felt about their building and their past. It alerted attention to the remarkable and highly evocative semi-circular space that sat in the centre of the building, sometimes unnoticed behind closed doors. With its 298 numbered seats on the ground floor hall (each of them over the century allocated to a particular lodge) it spoke of a time when hundreds of men, the delegates from their lodges, would sit and listen and argue over the major issues of the day. A list from 1947 identified 150 of these seats and it was decided that an announcement would be made saying that:

> To raise money for the renovation of the pitman's parliament, we're launching a one-off sponsorship scheme... The minimum seat sponsorship is *£100* and all the money raised will go towards the Redhills renovation project.

Names and dedications would be added to the seats and the sponsors would be provided with a token. The response was incredible. Fifty thousand pounds was collected within a year and this paid for all of the seats to be reupholstered and maintained. But there was more involved than money. As with the 'marra', the process of identifying with a seat proved to be a deeply moving one as people arrived at Redhills with stories of family members, friends and lodge officials, bringing the past back to life. Several of the seats were overwhelmed with dedications in a process that seemed to return the building to the people.

This was one step along the road that would once again place the building, and with it the culture and politics of mining, at the centre of life in the city. As with the banner groups, the intervention had produced a dramatic emotional response, something that Forbes saw as 'a rising up of the people who were angered to have their culture taken away from them – a deep emotional attachment that is breath-taking'. The plan for Redhills envisages a creative working centre of activity based around the cultural production of brass band music and banner restoration. It would see the 'Pitman's Parliament' re-engaged as the site of argument and discussion fostering links with both Durham University and New College as a place of learning, practices and performance. It would be a cultural revolution and an authentic companion to the Big Meeting extending the changes that had followed the strike in 1985.

In conclusion

The Gala that took place in 2018 – the one that Amber A' Lee Frost had travelled to attend – attracted a huge attendance. She had spoken at the customary UNITE summer school the evening before and there was the normally large delegation from that union and many others. Jeremy Corbyn as leader of the Labour Party was once again the main speaker reversing the established trend under New Labour. In the previous year, his speech had been interrupted by a drunken woman who had clambered onto the stage in an attempt to talk with him. This alerted the DMA to the need for greater security and prompted a full examination of the way in which the speakers' platform was organised and the speeches relayed to the gathered crowd. A new professional stage was in place in 2018 along with new sound equipment and large screens. George Robson commented that: "For the first time in a hundred years the people will be able to see the speakers and hear what they are saying." Others asked, "Why didn't we think of doing this before?" But it was done and, alongside everything else, it provided a strong signal that – yet again – the Gala was here to stay as an established trade union and community event, affirming the value of collective action and giving support to socialist ideas and causes.

NOTES

(1) *https://thebaffler.com/all-tomorrows-parties/nostalgia-mining-frost*

(2) For an account of the importance of Gresford and the life of Robert Saint see Crookston (2010)

(3) In fact it was earlier than this, in 1947 they started arriving at 7 a.m.

(4) *The Big Meeting* can be viewed at www. huwbeynoin.com/media. In November 1983 I showed it at a national NUM School at Wortley Hall in Yorkshire. It was attended by delegates from across the coalfields and I was surprised when, in discussion, the men from Nottinghamshire said that they found it very hard to relate to, that it was in some way beyond their experience. It made me think that more should have been done to involve the Nottingham lodges in the event.

(5) These issues are developed further in a book with my friend Ray Hudson, *The Shadow of the Mine: Coal and the end of Industrial Britain* Verso, 2020,

(6) *www.amber-online.com/collections/miners-weekend-school-1984d*

(7) Grahame Morris resigned in 2018 and was replaced by David Anderson, former miner and former MP of Blaydon

REFERENCES

Ayre, D. (1979) "Instinctive Socialism" in T. Austrin, et.al., But the World Goes on the Same: Changing times in Durham pit Villages, *Strong Words*, Whitley Bay, pp. 7-14

Beynon, H. (2017) "A Challenging Life: Dave Hopper 1943-2016", in G. Williams , *The Flame Still Burns*, Campaign for Press and Broadcasting Freedom, Nottingham, pp 7-12

Crookstone, P. (2010) *The Pitman's Requiem*, Northumbria Press, Newcastle upon Tyne

Durham Miner, 17, 2016 *www.durhamminer-org/publications*

Robson, G. (2010) "The Gala's about Heritage" in P. Crookston, *The Pitman's Requiem*, Northumbria Press, Newcastle upon Tyne, pp 65-69

Stephenson, C. and Wray, D. (2005) 'Emotional Regeneration through Community Action in Post-industrial Mining Communities: The New Herrington Miners' Banner Partnership', *Capital and Class*, 87, 175–199

Temple, 2012: *The Big Meeting: A History of the Durham Miners' Gala.* TUPS Books, Washington, Tyne and Wear.

Death knell for deep mining revealed in 1992 cabinet records
Nicholas Jones

A belated apology by John Major for the devastation caused by the 1992 pit closure programme came within months of National Archives releasing cabinet papers that revealed a twisted tale of blatant ministerial duplicity and subterfuge within Downing Street and Whitehall. Major finally admitted that his handling of what resulted in the demise of the coal industry had been the 'biggest single misjudgement' of his Premiership. To hasten privatisation of British Coal, the government's financial advisers Rothschilds had secretly planned the shutdown of 31 pits in contravention of review procedures for colliery closures. Michael Heseltine, who had only recently taken over as President of the Board of Trade, had secured Treasury approval for £1 billion in redundancy payments, confident in his belief that 30,000 miners destined to lose their jobs would take the money rather than fight the closures. His justification for such a drastic cut in output was that there was 'no market for anything other than a fraction of British deep-mined coal' because electricity generators could buy coal far cheaper on the world market.

Heseltine was greeted with uproar in the House of Commons and the country when he announced the closures, some to take effect immediately in October 1992. Behind the scenes there had been infighting within cabinet, and, amid the chaos and confusion that ensued, the Prime Minister ordered Heseltine to make a rapid and embarrassing U-turn. Some pits won a short-term reprieve, but the closures were to become a point of no return for British coalfields, the eventual death knell for deep mining. The cabinet papers indicated that Downing Street's policy unit was in no doubt where blame lay for the botched announcement: Heseltine had been hoping to 'take the credit for the next popular privatisation' but discovered that he was about to act as 'the undertaker to the coal industry'.

Major acknowledged his misjudgement in September 2018 during a speech in South Shields, where Westoe, the last Tyne and Wear pit – and one of the 31 listed by Heseltine – closed in May 1993. He admitted his government had failed to pump sufficient money into former coalfields for the industrial regeneration that was needed. Major tried to reach out to a former coalfield community where so many jobs had been lost: "We were not a bunch of monsters with vile intentions." In an interview he gave me in December 2017, to coincide with the publication of the 1992 cabinet records, Heseltine owned up to failings on his own part. He had been unthinking in his approach for not having understood the depth of public sympathy for mining communities, especially in south-east of England, but he still had no regrets about the decisions he had taken. He had mounted an equally staunch defence of the logic behind his action two years earlier when I interviewed him at the time of the closure in December 2015 of Kellingley in Yorkshire, the very last deep pit. His argument was that in 1992 he could not ignore the fall-out from a rapidly changing energy market: gas-fired electricity generation was increasing, and generators were turning away from coal mined in the UK because the cost was far higher than world prices.

"I did everything within my legal and reasonable powers to persuade them, but they simply said we can buy coal cheaper on the markets and no deal was done, so there was no market for anything other than a fraction of British deep-mined coal. That led me to the uncomfortable, controversial decision that I had to close 31 pits." (Michael Heseltine, BBC Newsnight, 13.8.2015)

Heseltine's stark personal assessment of the bleak prospects for the coal industry is repeated on page after page of the 1992 cabinet records: closures were said to be unavoidable because of 'the remorseless pressure of the market decline for coal'. But the archives also revealed the lack of thought, let alone concern, for the long-term future of coalfield communities. The priority was to slim down British Coal – successor to the National Coal Board – as fast as possible so that the most profitable remaining pits could be sold off rapidly to the private sector. A quick sale would be achieved through the short-term fix of offering redundancy payments averaging £30,000 per miner.

Reaction to Heseltine's announcement was so swift and savage that within days 200,000 people marched through London in protest at the decimation of coalfield communities; national newspapers which had demonised the NUM President Arthur Scargill during the 1984-85 strike, declared him a hero for fighting back; and once individual pits were named and under notice, there was a concerted wave of protest action organised by Women Against Pit Closures.

Major had promoted Heseltine to become President of the Board of Trade after the Conservatives won the general election of April 1992. He inherited work already set in process by his predecessor John Wakeham, the former Secretary of State for Energy. Wakeham had overseen privatisation of the 12 regional electricity companies in December 1990 and had begun preparing for privatisation of British Coal. The 1992 cabinet papers expose the scale of the secret steps that had been taken to slim down the industry and how, in the aftermath of the shock announcement, there was a flurry of confidential Downing Street memos that contained excoriating criticism of Heseltine for mishandling public sympathy for the miners, and for generating a flood of accusations of government 'betrayal' of men in the Nottinghamshire coalfield, who had stayed loyal to Margaret Thatcher in the 1984-85 pit strike. Major was forced within days to order an immediate inquiry into energy policy.

The cabinet records identified two significant failings on Heseltine's part: he had relied on 'unsatisfactory' advice from Rothschilds and both he and his financial consultants were at fault for not keeping abreast of the law on colliery closures. Preparations for privatising British Coal had been accelerated because new coal contracts had to be signed within months with electricity generators and a deal seemed unlikely because deep-mined coal could not compete with imports. Rothschilds' recommendation was that 31 of the 50 pits should be closed, reducing the headcount of miners from 54,000 to 24,000. Those collieries that remained should be sold off as two separate companies.

By July 1992 the argument among cabinet ministers revolved around the scale of redundancy payments that would be needed. Michael Portillo, chief secretary to the Treasury, backed by the Chancellor of the Exchequer, Norman Lamont, wanted to cap the redundancy pay-off at £350 million. Heseltine demanded far more generous terms, arguing that the government should buy out the risk of another pit strike. British Coal had proposed that each miner should be paid from £35,000 to £42,000, at a cost to the Treasury of nearly £1.3 billion. Heseltine supported higher pay-offs because British Coal was about to impose compulsory redundancies and abandon safeguards in the colliery review procedure because on current coal prices 'virtually none of British Coal's mines would be immediately viable'.

Lamont agreed to go to £720 million, although he thought that was still 'too lavish', but Heseltine insisted that unless redundant men got the equivalent of two years' pay, there could be a backlash. "This could all too easily create a sense of betrayal, particularly among UDM miners in Nottinghamshire, who this time will be harder hit than NUM miners in Yorkshire." Heseltine backed up his case with warnings from pit managers about the impact of abolishing the colliery review procedure and the loss of the chance for men to opt to work at other pits. "British Coal say unattractive terms will lead to a collapse in morale, strikes, possible industrial vandalism, and perhaps civil disorder." As late as mid-September there had still been no agreement. The Treasury said the country could not afford Heseltine's latest estimate of £1.1 billion and warned that the government should not be 'blackmailed by threats of strike action'.

There had been rumours earlier in the year that British Coal was planning to scale back production. Arthur Scargill had published leaked documents suggesting that more pit closures were likely, and as the Nottinghamshire coalfield faced substantial closures, Major had taken the precaution of holding a meeting with Roy Lynk, President of the rival Union of Democratic Mineworkers, whose members had continued working during the 1984-85 strike. A Downing Street note preparing Major for his meeting warned closures would be 'particularly unpalatable' in Nottinghamshire, and that miners might feel they were being treated unfairly. The UDM was principally concerned about lack of alternative employment rather than redundancy terms. "The effect on UDM areas would be devastating. British Coal Enterprises would be unable to provide new employment opportunities to match the scale of the redundancies. Areas such as Mansfield, where the 1984 strike had been resisted, would have a 20 per cent unemployment level. Many parts of the East Midlands would become industrial wasteland: about 12,000 miners, currently earning £20,000 on average, would be made redundant."

At his meeting with the Prime Minister, Lynk

complained about being described by Scargill as 'a puppet of the government', and said he sensed the UDM was losing ground in the Nottinghamshire coalfield. A Downing Street account of the conversation noted that Lynk feared ten pits might close and that he had asked for more support for creating new employment opportunities: "It would be important to co-ordinate better all the agencies dealing with regeneration …The Prime Minister expressed his concern about the many small communities dependent on mines that would close. What would be the impact? 'Horrific' said Mr Lynk."

On the eve of his statement in the House of Commons – on 13 October 1992 –Heseltine was reminded by Portillo that he should stick to the figure the Treasury agreed: the redundancy pay-off for 30,000 miners would cost 'up to a billion'. In the event the size of the pay-off was not the issue. Next day's newspapers were dominated by reports of 'nightmare' news for the coalfields. 'Savage government axe kills 30,000 mining jobs' was *The Guardian*'s front page headline. Although *The Guardian* acknowledged that the £1 billion package to fund compulsory redundancies was the most 'generous on offer', Heseltine was criticised for failing to say how much had been set aside in employment support for the mining communities.

Such was the outrage in the Conservative Party at the betrayal of the UDM that Major was forced to call an emergency cabinet meeting that agreed within days to re-phase the closures. Ten of the 31 pits were taken off the list, and the other 21 closures delayed for a full review into their viability. 'Hezza's U-turn on pits' was *The Sun*'s headline. 'Major's Pit Stop' was blazoned across the *Daily Mirror*'s front page report on the Prime Minister's 'sensational and humiliating climbdown'.

What newspapers were to dub 'The Great Tory Revolt' had Heseltine as its target: 'hundreds of *The Sun*'s readers' sent messages of support to Roy Lynk urging a Conservative government to remember its debt to the Nottinghamshire coalfield. "Two million lights went out across Britain last night as people flicked a switch to support the miners." Miners from Frickley in Yorkshire dumped a lorry load of coal to block the gates to Heseltine's country estate under a banner declaring, 'Coal Not Dole. Frickley NUM. Up Yours!'

Such was the anger among Conservative MPs that Major faced possible defeat in an emergency Commons debate. Heseltine was forced into his second climbdown within three days with an announcement of a wide-ranging review into government energy policy to investigate whether the energy market had been 'rigged' against coal. 'Tories struggle home with 13-vote majority on pits' said the front-page headline of *The Times* over its report of a stormy debate in which six Conservative MPs voted with the Opposition and another five abstained. Filling all the front pages that morning were pictures of a march through London organised by the NUM, to coincide with the critical parliamentary vote, which attracted 100,000 protestors and drew support from across the capital. Twice as many attended the TUC's mass rally in Hyde Park the following Sunday.

Even though I have spent much of my career trying to keep abreast of the highs and lows of the coal industry, I found it a humbling experience digging into my files and turning over newspaper front pages for 22 and 26 October 1992. If only the miners and their union had been able to win over the right-wing press in the way they did that week, Margaret Thatcher might well have been forced to negotiate her way out of the 1984-85 strike.

Almost filling *The Sun*'s front page was a photograph of 'a mighty army of miners' whose march for coal and jobs 'won the support of Britain's diehard Tories'. To the paper's evident surprise even 'Sloane Rangers left their tables at swanky eateries and customers poured from posh boutiques in Kensington and Chelsea to wave them on'. 'Pit leader Scargill is mobbed by admirers as smiling police look on' said the caption to the *Daily Mirror*'s front-page picture. 'In swanky Park Lane, an admirer handed Scargill a bouquet of white chrysanthemums.' Instead of the invective of the 1980s, *The Sun*'s editorial reflected the mood on the streets: "The miners' conduct yesterday was exemplary. They are men of honour." For the *Daily Mail* it had been a day of 'quiet dignity' when miners and their families brought their 'peaceful protest to London' in 'marked contrast to the ugly, violent scenes which characterised the 1984 strike'.

As Major picked himself up after the rebellion, and Heseltine set in motion arrangements for the inquiry into the energy market, an inquest was launched in Downing Street to work out how to recover the initiative. The depth of anger among Major's colleagues and aides over the botched announcement was all too evident. "We have lost the emotional and economic argument," said one note to the Prime Minister the day before the vote. David Poole, an adviser in the policy unit, had some blunt advice for Major: "The principal lesson to be learned from this episode when dealing with issues of policy is that one should not fall into the trap of assuming that ministers and officials know what they are doing or have thought it through." Major was told by Poole that he should be 'buttonholing' Heseltine to get a clear steer as to whether the review was simply designed to 'smooth the way towards the eventual implementation' of an interrupted pit closure policy.

Keith Loader, private secretary to Heseltine, wrote back to reassure the Prime Minister that the department was proposing a 'genuine' review into the 21 named pits and this would consider 'social and economic implications of further pit closures' as well as options to 'increase coal burn'. Poole wasn't convinced. He feared Heseltine wanted to re-phase redundancies over two or three years as a way of reducing the number of miners put out of work simultaneously. Another suspicion was that Heseltine was angling to keep the proportion of coal burned higher than would be the case were there a competitive market. "Any option to increase coal burn will involve direct interference in the electricity market."

Heseltine was also criticised for leaving it until the day of his announcement before informing fellow ministers of the names of the 31 pits listed for closure. Some didn't realise that Point of Ayr colliery was in North Wales and not Scotland. A copy of Heseltine's parliamentary statement was sent to Downing Street the day before, but pits were not named. Such was the fear of leaks and Whitehall's distrust of British Coal that other departments had been purposely kept in the dark. This had contributed to 'widespread failure to foresee the strength of public reaction,' said Sir Peter Gregson, who was asked by the Cabinet Office to discover why so little was known in advance. David Poole assessed the reasons for the confusion in the policy unit's confidential report, 'The Pit Closure Episode'. He concluded that the closure announcement took on its own momentum because officials 'over relied' on Rothschilds' advice and failed to stop and ask themselves whether announcing 31 closures altogether remained a sensible option. This failure was compounded by the fact that at this critical moment the Department of Energy had been merged with the Department for Trade and Industry. Poole believed this was where the fault lay:

This was just when the coal industry needed a senior and politically sensitive cabinet minister who wholly understood the detail not just of pit closures but also the electricity industry, its key players and their inter-action to the electricity and coal market places. Unfortunately, Michael Heseltine did not meet these criteria. Furthermore, I have come to believe that he was simply unable to bring himself to face up to the truth of what it was that he was being required to do. Rather than being about to take the credit for the next major popular privatisation he discovered that he was to act as the undertaker to the coal industry. At no point until the crisis broke did he properly engage himself in what was taking place.

Increasingly ministers and officials became mesmerised by the detail of the process and failed to stand back in order to keep the wider context and implications in view. When therefore the announcement of the pit closures programme became a lightning conductor for national fears, no one was adequately prepared. The department allowed themselves to be rolled over by British Coal who ran an effective and highly destructive public relations campaign designed to shift blame from themselves and on to the government.

Poole believed Heseltine should have been alerted to the political dangers that lay ahead when Arthur Scargill published leaked documents suggesting that pit closures were being planned. "We allowed ourselves to be lulled by our muted response to Scargill's leak .... There was a complete failure of political sensitivity at exactly the time it was needed." When this criticism was put to Heseltine 25 years later, he acknowledged he had been remiss. In an interview for BBC Radio's *UK Confidential* in December 2017 he explained why he had been caught off-guard by the outcry that greeted news of 31 pit closures: "I thought that this was not going to be the great shock that I had previously thought it might be."

A willingness within Whitehall to flout the requirements of the colliery review procedures was another issue tackled by the policy unit. Poole suggested an inquiry into the role of financial advisers Rothschilds with whom blame should lie for not exercising due diligence and for the 'quality and breadth of their advice'. "Something must be done to signal a reaction to unsatisfactory work, particularly by financial advisers in the City who charge government very substantial fees."

Objectives were finally agreed for the energy review ordered by Heseltine, but again cabinet papers underline cynicism behind his U-turn. He asked for advice on how British Coal could compete with imports to 'ensure coal can be returned to the private sector as soon as possible'. Privatisation was to remain the priority while attempting at the same time to 'save enough pits to satisfy the political expectations underlying the review'. When presented with the findings, Heseltine concluded that the 'energy market was not rigged against coal'; that British Coal was not competitive; that 25 to 35 pit closures were inevitable; and that he favoured a four to five-year transition with subsidies to British Coal 'to allow phased pit closures at the lower end'.

In parliamentary terms, Heseltine could argue that he had fulfilled undertakings he had given MPs: there had been a reprieve for ten of the 31 pits and an extensive review into the energy market which had justified the need for closures. While complexities surrounding competing price structures of coal, gas and electricity passed most people by, there was a widespread suspicion that the public had been misled and the unfairness of what was happening was plain to see: pits were being decimated out of political and commercial expediency. Wilful destruction of great industries and their workforces was rapidly turning Thatcher into a hate figure in Britain's industrial heartlands and as Heseltine had found to his cost, that shared sense of loss had finally crossed the class divide. Consciences had been well and truly stirred in the prosperous south-east of England where the miners' plight had come to symbolise growing unease over the social cost of wanton industrial vandalism.

Political activism by miners' wives, forged in the 1984-85 strike at soup kitchens and food banks, re-asserted itself once closures took effect. Women Against Pit Closures organised marches, sit-ins and pit camps in an attempt to protect coalfield jobs. A pit occupation at Parkside colliery in Lancashire, led by Anne Scargill, inspired Maxine Peake to write her play *Queens of the Coal Age*, her tribute to the politicising of women in the mining communities. At some pits, miners' wives displayed greater fervour than their husbands, but Heseltine's prediction about take-up for his £1 billion pay-off would prove to be correct. When faced by redundancy, the prospect of a cash payment was all-too tempting to reject and closures went ahead one by one. By December 1993, Heseltine was finally in a position to unveil his legislation privatising the industry.

Nonetheless it begged the question: if it was possible to force Major's government on to the defensive through the combined pressure of two demonstrations, a backbench revolt and a critical media, why had the NUM been unable to mobilise that same level of support when it mattered most of all in 1984? Any wishful thinking on my part had to be tempered by the grim reality of what I heard in the lead-up to privatisation. In December 1994, at the final lunch for industrial correspondents given by the British Coal chairman, I sat next to Kevan Hunt, director of employee relations. My note of what he said encapsulated the death throes of a once great industry:

We saw Michael Heseltine in the summer of 1992, just before he announced the closure of 31 pits that October. He refused point blank to stop the dash-for-gas although forty coal-fired power stations had already been closed. The Conservatives dropped the ban on burning gas for generating electricity in 1990. Gas stations are much cheaper to build and are much more profitable… We knew a future Labour government could not do anything because the privatised regional electricity companies cannot be forced to burn coal …. I don't think there is any chance of a comeback. Even if coal for oil becomes a proposition, it will be done in Australia where coal reserves are so cheap ….

We knew the moment we met Heseltine that the coal industry was finished. He said the dash-for-gas had been a great commercial success. We could see Heseltine liked the political freedom it had given the Conservatives. I think he could have saved the industry if only he had been willing to stop the dash for gas.

'It has to be a miner's wife!'
Representing women in mining activism
Jean Spence and Carol Stephenson

'One of us'

THE VANE TEMPEST WOMEN'S VIGIL began on a cold
January morning in 1993. It was one of seven women's pit
camps established outside threatened collieries in response
to the announcement in October 1992 that 31 out of 50
remaining deep mine pits were earmarked for closure, with
the projected loss of 31,000 jobs.

I joined the women gathering outside the pit that morning
determined that however much the odds were against us,
we should campaign to stop this closure programme. I
did worry that we might be fighting a losing battle, but,
whatever the odds, the point was to fight it. In the wake
of the viciousness and injustices served upon miners, their
families, and supporters during and after the 1984-85 strike,
I wanted to show that 'my people' would not be cowed and
that we still had the will to struggle for what we believed to
be right. By 'my people' I meant mining people, and anyone
else whose politics were sympathetic to the miners' cause.
Women joined the vigil from a variety of backgrounds.
They included mining family members, students,
professional and creative workers, Labour Party activists,
unaligned socialists and feminists. Some had been directly
involved in the strike. Others hadn't. I was able to
participate because study leave from my job as a community
and youth work lecturer meant my time was my own
to organise. I came from a mining family, but my father
had died in 1980. I had supported the 1984-85 strike but
had not been centrally involved. I was not a miner's wife.
Taking part in the vigil was an expression of my own life
experiences and identity, but also, inseparable from that, I

177

was there because I understood the attack on mining jobs to be symptomatic of a broader attack on working class employment and organisation that had implications well beyond mining.

On the first morning of the vigil there was a large number of journalists present. I was completely taken aback when one reporter approached me to ask if she and her colleagues could visit my home the next day to film me getting up, getting my children ready for school and seeing my husband off to work. I was, and continue to be, perplexed by the range of assumptions contained in this request.

Later one of the women, married to an NUM leader, proclaimed that we had 'no connection with Greenham Common', declaring that we should emphasise that when speaking to the press. Given the positive links made between women strike activists and the Greenham women's peace camp, and that Greenham had provided the model for the pit camps, this seemed odd. I explained it to myself as a defensive response to the antagonism of the press to the Greenham action and to all things 'feminist'.[1] Still I was uncomfortable with the denial.

A number of us involved in the Vane Tempest Vigil were self-proclaimed socialist feminists. I had always thought of myself as a socialist, but encountering feminism had enabled me to make a visceral connection between my personal experiences as a miner's daughter and socialist politics. It was feminism that gave me the confidence to participate in the vigil. Moreover, it was because I had struggled against the gender expectations associated with being a miner's daughter that I was now in a position to participate. Yet that feminism was now put to one side in favour of my identity as a miner's daughter. My credibility rested on my mining credentials rather than my political understanding. My 'belonging' was affirmed by one woman telling me 'you are one of us, you are!'. I was happy to belong, but again, perplexed by the exclusion of other relevant aspects of my being.

Since 1993, I have continued to reflect upon the significance of privileging my mining identity during the vigil.[2] This has extended into work with Carol Stephenson, and together we have used our female working class life experiences to analyse the impact of gender in mining life and politics.[3] In what follows, we use my experience of the Vane Tempest Vigil as a starting point for understanding the relevance of female mining identities to the strike and the vigil.

Jean Spence January 2019

Introduction

The question of identity permeates interest in women's activism within mining politics. It is implicit in requests from researchers and students to interview 'miner's wives' who were involved in the strike. It is foregrounded in commemorative events and articles that seek to honour women activists. It is central to characterisation in cultural productions representing the history of mining life and politics. Having been a miner, a miner's wife, a member of a miner's family, or, at a stretch, a member of a mining community, carries its own authority. Insofar as the narratives offered by individuals who can claim a mining identity are taken as authentic, they are regarded as self-explanatory and generally 'true'. Three instances from our encounters in recent years illustrate this: an academic speaker at a Working Class Studies conference offered the information that she was a miner's daughter to add weight to her analysis; a PhD student prioritised contact with miners' wives to access understanding of the Orgreave Truth and Justice campaign; a writer at a symposium presented the intergenerational stories of one female strike activist as representative of the history of all women in mining life.

Activist miners' wives have come to be seen as symbolic of the potential of all female working class struggle to create a better world. The ideal of the 'miner's wife' contains within it qualities such as loyalty, endurance, forbearance, selflessness. The activist wife is additionally brave and strong. Her commitment to justice and collective well-being exemplifies the values of working class organisation, socialism and trade unionism. Yet the narrative piquancy of these imputed virtues rests upon the historically unequal sexual division of labour in mining life in which the partnership between men and women was ultimately framed by male power. The designation 'miner's wife' contains implicit gendered constraints. In the miners' strike, these constraints were challenged by the realities of female activism that included typically 'feminist' strategies of independent organisation, decision-making, and action. The process of collective female activism involved conversation and consciousness-raising. However, to have acknowledged the feminist implications of this process would have disrupted the terms in which women could support the miners. In a predominantly male strike struggling for male jobs, led by the overwhelmingly male NUM, it was incumbent upon the women to manage gaps between expectation and reality in ways that did not challenge the masculine power of mining. Foregrounding the leadership of 'miners' wives' and a particular trajectory of activism in representing the women's struggle was a useful mechanism for achieving this.[4]

The strike

The story of female involvement in the 1984-85 strike is well rehearsed. Briefly, large numbers of women from mining families, many of whom had not previously been politically active, came out in support of the strike. They used their traditional domestic skills to feed striking miners and their families, but eventually transcended the limits of domesticity by becoming involved in all areas of the struggle. The strike was a defining moment for them, precipitating a new way of being in the world. After a gruelling year ending in a return to work with no gains, it was the strength, determination and continuing activism of the women in political and community arenas that offered a message of hope for the future. Understandably, it is the stories of the women who best fit this narrative that have come to the fore in the years since the strike. Such women are persistently revisited by the press, by researchers and by creative producers interested in recalling the strike.[5]

Yet that is the story of only one group of women. Women strike activists came from different backgrounds, and with different skills and interests. Some miners' wives were there because their husbands were in union leadership roles. Some already had a background of political and community activism. Others went back to traditional roles after the strike. Women who had no immediate connections with mining became involved because of their political affiliations or because they recognised the miners' struggle as representative of their own sectional concerns. Accounts of a range of women activists appear in a number of publications in the wake of the strike.[6] There are, of course, stories unheard. The strike legacy includes despair as well as hope, shame as well as heroism, individualism, cynicism and self-delusion as well as collectivism and political engagement and a fight for justice. The experiences of women in mining families who endured the strike without becoming actively involved largely remain in the private sphere. There is a silence from those wives who supported their husbands in strike breaking. Even some published accounts slip from view as audiences make moral or political decisions regarding which stories they seek, choose to hear, or authenticate.

Whatever the complexities, it was women from mining

families who, organising themselves as women, initially to meet the need for food, care, and mutual support in the conditions of the strike, precipitated the wider women's strike movement. They were the women personally experiencing the hardship, the injustices of the benefits system, the victimisation and criminalisation perpetrated by massed ranks of police marching into their localities, and the lies being perpetrated by the media.[7] It is not surprising that these women were called upon to 'bear witness'. The authenticity of their experiences as mining women was integral to the truth of their accounts. Helpfully, in a febrile anti-socialist climate, as miners' wives they were assumed to have no ideological axe to grind. Their personal experiences could not be easily dismissed or vilified. Even antagonists might see them as 'innocent' victims, acting, as women should, in defence of their husbands, their families and neighbourhoods. As such, conforming to expectations about what it meant to be a miner's wife had a public relations value.[8]

To positively promote the miners' cause, members of the women's support groups needed to be seen to be 'ordinary, respectable women'. They had well-founded concerns that the media would pick up on any opportunity to bring them into disrepute and they worried that outsiders, such as middle class feminists or members of political fringe groups, would infiltrate the women's groups to pursue their own (diversionary) agendas – as indeed some tried to – or that middle class do-gooders would take over. So, for example, only women who were related to miners could claim membership of the Eppleton Miners' Wives Support Group.[9] Meanwhile, in North Staffordshire, a 'political decision' was made to name the support group a 'Miners' Wives Action Group even though not all of those involved could claim that identity.[10] Nationally, Women Against Pit Closures decreed that the organisation should comprise

75% miners' families: the remainder to be invited outsiders recognised as having offered special support. Maintaining the leadership of women from mining families was a means whereby their voices could remain at the centre. It thus facilitated the development of their skills, helped them gain confidence and crucially, sustained the partnership with miners and their union.

Clearly there were practical and justifiable reasons for privileging mining identities during the strike. Miners' wives became the cause célèbre of the movement because of the pivotal position that they inhabited in reality and because of the ideal image of the working class wife that they represented. However, not all the consequences were positive.

Firstly, it is conceivable that in some mining districts, there were sympathetic women who were discouraged from helping. Unless they could find an alternative mechanism through which they could organise – such as a union or sympathetic Labour Party branch – not being able to claim a mining identity was a disincentive. Nevertheless, as the strike progressed, increasing numbers of different women did become involved, sometimes through their professional roles, e.g. as welfare rights' or community workers. These women made a significant and well-acknowledged contribution.[11] Yet with the passage of time, they have been increasingly marginalised by commentators obsessed with miners' wives, and are gradually being 'hidden from history'.[12]

Secondly, female employees of the NCB, themselves on strike as trade unionists, were caught between the male dominated NUM and the Women's Support Groups. On the margins of both, their interests were underplayed and many seem to have returned to work before the strike ended.[13] Conversely, many of the women involved in support groups as wives were already committed trade unionists.[14] That this aspect of their identity was consistently underplayed did nothing to encourage female trade unionism at a time when all unions, especially in the powerful, male dominated industrial sector, were under attack and when the feminisation of the workforce that was already underway, was largely non-unionised. Relating to this, the emergent political consciousness amongst women who were miners' wives or relations offered an opportunity for the politicisation of the neighbourhood and community sphere, suggesting opportunities for the development of community and trade union links that were blocked by the imaginary representation of the male worker and his dependent wife.

Thirdly, the provision of food by mining women reasserted a tradition of female domesticity that no longer mapped directly onto the realities of mining families in 1980s Britain. Even if the feeding of strikers and their families was the priority of the women, doing so involved more than cooking. At minimum, organisational and fund-raising skills were necessary to success. The communal kitchens themselves acted as a hub of organisation and information exchange between all who used them, creating an intense political learning environment that encouraged some women to join the picket lines and to broaden their strike strategies. The constraints of traditional expectations associated with being a miner's wife were bound to be broken in such conditions. Political innocence, even if it had been present at the start would be dispelled in the course of the strike. Yet stereotypes lingered, as the following poem *The Pat on the Head* implies:

Here she is, come and see her
The pet miner's wife, she's over there.
No, not her, the one in red,
The one that looks underfed.

It's amazing, isn't it,
The way she's so articulate?
She really knows what she's about.

It's not just grunt, scream and shout.

I've heard she can do joined up writing,
Don't you think that's exciting?
Do you think she can read as well?
Ooh I don't know, you never can tell.

Well, it's been an eye opener coming here tonight,
You know, this miner's wife is quite bright.
I didn't pat her on the head,
She patted me on mine instead.

Written for Liz Hollis.[15]

The ideal of the miner's wife forced women activists who were wives into a position where it was necessary either to 'perform' to the expected role, in order to gain sympathy and support, or to risk losing that support by challenging preconceived ideas. Meanwhile, those who were not miners' wives needed to 'prove' themselves. The issue of identity, cohering around relationship with a miner, pervaded the discourse of female strike activism to the extent that all women were forced to manage the presentation of their activism through this filter. The process was to continue beyond the strike and to impact on the women's vigils of 1993.

The Vane Tempest Vigil
In the seven years between the end of the strike and the pit closure announcement, 125 pits were closed and 120,000 mining jobs lost.[16] The fears that had precipitated the strike had been more than realised. Conditions for all working people had deteriorated. In some areas, unemployment was endemic as de-industrialisation destroyed traditional working class jobs. Enterprising individualism was the order the day. Anti-union legislation was shackling workers

*Seaham WAPC and the Vane Tempest Vigil banners on the London march,
27 March 1993*

and a relentless assault on the welfare state was adding to the impoverishment of swathes of working class families.[17]

Vane Tempest, now threatened with closure, was the last of Seaham's three pits. Like other localities founded on coal mining, the town was struggling to reinvent itself. Expanding numbers of care homes employing low paid, female labour could hardly compensate for the decline in mining. The desire to fight the pit closure programme was strong but compromised by 'realistic' assessments of what was possible: for many miners and their families, the chance to take enhanced redundancy to facilitate the pit closure programme was a temptation that they could not ignore.

The organisation of a women's camp outside Vane Tempest was a last ditch effort to save the pit, but it also had symbolic value. The hope that the government's decision might be reversed was accompanied by a determination to resist, and to be seen to resist, to be defying the defeat of the strike. Inevitably echoes and memories of the strike pervaded both the actions of those protesting and the responses of the public. Across the UK there was an outpouring of public sympathy, including unambiguous support from the Labour Party leadership and fellow trade unionists, such as had never been the case during the strike.[18] The sympathy was encouraging but with hindsight it might be perceived as an indulgent and sentimental response to the death throes of a once mighty industry. Sentimentalism fed stereotypes, including those concerning the nature of work in the pit, the idea of 'mining community', and of 'miners' wives' that had never been significantly challenged in the strike.

There was both continuity and discontinuity between female strike activism and the women's vigils. The vigils operated under the auspices of Women Against Pit Closures, and the experiences and example of the women of the strike was ever-present. The women did not need to justify their presence and from the outset it was assumed that they were

187

capable and would work together constructively for the common cause of saving jobs in mining. It was assumed that the NUM and its decisions would be respected. In their turn, the women's efforts were acknowledged by miners and their families, and local people associated with mining both visited the caravan at Vane Tempest and participated in events that the vigil women organised.

However, the vigil was not the strike. Nobody was hungry. There were no pickets. The police were 'hands off'. The positive reasons for maintaining the centrality of mining identity in the campaign were absent. Only two Vane Tempest miners' wives were involved. Yet the idea of the miner's wife persisted in external assumptions that the majority of the women involved in the vigil were 'supporting their husbands'. On the contrary, most of the women took part either because they had connections with the local NUM leadership and the Labour Party, and/or because of their political understanding of the implications of the closure programme. Yet the miners' wife trope was never resisted. This put a particular burden upon those who could claim such an identity – they were consistently projected into the limelight in order to promote the authenticity of the campaign. Meanwhile, other voices were subdued. One of the miner's wives involved, who also held a responsible management position in the NHS, summed up the pressure to perform in her poem *We need a Speaker:*

There are seven little words
That filled me with dread
And almost every time we met
I heard them said

I understand the reasons
And had to agree
As a group it did give us
More credibility.

Nevertheless those words
I'll remember for all my life
Yes, you've guessed
'We need a speaker:
IT HAS TO BE A MINER'S WIFE!' [19]

Thus the motivation for female participation in the vigil was consistently represented as personal. It was the personal experience and understanding of the women involved that was sought and offered. This might have facilitated a positive connection with the feminist idea that the personal is political, but because it was filtered through the lens of female mining identity, it actually reaffirmed unequal gender relationships. In the process of personalisation, political understanding was de-centred. Local representatives of the NUM never sought the opinions of the Vane Tempest women formally or informally, about the direction of the campaign against pit closures. At the end of the campaign, after Vane Tempest closed and the caravan was towed to Durham for the Miners' Gala, the women were invited onto the speakers' platform to sing, but not to speak. The honour was refused on the grounds that the women's role was not that of entertainers.

The reiteration of the trope of the miner's wife, seriously underplayed the extent of women's capacity for independent thought and action outside mining identity. It subdued the coherent socialist and feminist views of the majority of the women involved in the vigil and thus blocked opportunities to promote a wider vision of socialism and trade unionism relevant to changing conditions. By obstructing feminist influence, it ignored the political potential of organising in civil society around issues that were not immediately work-related but which had implications for trade unionism. The denial of feminism in the vigil locked the miners' campaign against pit closures into a conservative view of struggle, located in historic models that obstructed the possibility of working towards different futures beyond the demise of mining.

The slogan adopted by the women in Seaham – 'Jobs, community and environment' – encompassed complex ideas about the interrelationship between the three elements but not in romantic or idealist terms. Rather, the women were seeking a comprehensive approach to policy-making around mining with wider implications for the future. All that was a fundamental challenge to the ways in which neo-liberal policy-making was proceeding, but it was also a fundamental challenge to assumptions ingrained within the masculine labour and trade union movements which betrayed an inability to move beyond received wisdom about the nature of work, social and family organisation and political strategy.

Conclusion

Following the complete closure of deep coal mining in the UK, sentimentalism has, if anything, become more pervasive. It is ingrained in public art, in museums and in the continuous call for 'authentic' mining voices, especially those involved in the strike, to tell their stories. In this process, the radical politics of the strike, and the subsequent campaign against pit closures are becoming atrophied, their implications for present thinking and radical alternatives neutralised. The organisation of working class women in the strike and the political commitment represented in the vigils held glimpses of new ways of organising around class issues – making links across sectional interests, between unions and communities, between formal and informal decision-making processes and including men and women as partners in the process. However, the dependence upon authentic identities as exemplified by the trope of the 'miner's wife' deflected attention from the radical potential inherent in the women's activism. The ideals that persist in the notion of the 'miner's wife' must be acknowledged as ultimately politically conservative. Reifying mining identities dissipated female energy and insight and undermined female organisation, leaving only individuals, and small groups of women, operating in their own spheres of influence to carry forward gains they made in the strike.

NOTES

(1) Stead, J. *Never the same again: women and the miners' strike*. The Women's Press, 1987. Ch. 3.

(2) Spence, J. 'Women, Wives and the Campaign Against Pit Closures in County Durham: Understanding the Vane Tempest Vigil' in *Feminist Review*, 60, (1), 1996. pp 33–60.

(3) Stephenson's family background is in the steel industry in Consett. See for example, Spence, J. and Stephenson, C. 'Side by side with our men?' Women's activism, community and gender in the 1984-5 British Miners' Strike, *International Labour and Working Class History*, 75, 2009. pp.68-84.

(4) Allen, M. *Carrying on the Strike: The Politics of Women Against Pit Closures into 1990s* Ph.D Thesis, University of Manchester, 2000.

(5) Independent, 'Lessons from the University of Life', 16.2.95; *Daily Mirror,* 'The brave women who battled to keep Britain's coal mines open' 9.2.2014; Suddick, A. 'The past we inherit, the future we build', *Capital and Class,* 87, Autumn 2005.

(6) Stead op cit.; Seddon, V. (ed) *The Cutting Edge: Women and the Pit Strike.* London, Lawrence and Wishart, 1986.

(7) Williams, G. (ed) *Shafted: The Media, the Miners and the Aftermath.* Campaign for Press and Broadcasting Freedom, 2009.

(8) Allen, op cit.

(9) Stead, op cit. pp 18, 29.

(10) Bridget Bell, Forum Discussion, Northumbria University Conference. *The Miners' Strike, 20 Years On* 12.7.2004.

(11) Seddon, V. op. cit.

(12) Rowbotham, S. *Hidden from History. 300 Years of Women's Oppression and the Fight against It.* Pluto Press, 1975.

(13) Jackson, B. 'I am woman, I am strong!' in Allsop, D., Stephenson, C. and Wray, D. (eds) *Justice Denied: Friends, Foes and the Miners' Strike,* Merlin, 2017. pp. 24-37. See also, Dolby, N. Norma *Dolby's Diary: an account of the great miners' strike.* Verso. London, 1987.

(14) eg. *Sunderland Echo* 'Women at War', 12.3.2004. pp32-33.

(15) Lynne Dennet in Witham, J. *Hearts and Minds: The Story of the Women of Nottinghamshire in the Miners' Strike,* 1984-5 Canary Press, 1986. p143.

(16) SWAPC *You Can't Kill the Spirit! Houghton Main Pit Camp, South Yorkshire: the untold story of the women who set up camp to stop pit closures.* Northern Creative Print Solutions, 2018. pp14-15.

(17) Todd, S. *The People: the rise and fall of the working class, 1910-2010,* John Murray, 2014.

(18) See newspaper extracts in SWAPC op cit. pp.27,34,36.

(19) Gail Price (1993) in WAPC *The Vigil,* Heritage Coast Partnership, 2017. p12.

'You Can't Kill the Spirit', Sheffield Women Against Pit Closures

Caroline Poland, Debbie Matthews, Flis Callow and Marilyn Haddington

This chapter celebrates the key role played by women in fighting the continued destruction of coal mining communities in 1992-93. Many people know something about women against pit closures (WAPC) at the time of the year-long miners' strike of 1984-85. However, the story of how many of the same women came back together in 1992, joined by many others, to once again fight for jobs and communities, and against injustice, has been largely a hidden part of the history of activism.

Two recent publications by Women Against Pit Closures groups and a play by Maxine Peake are redressing this. This article is based on one of these publications, *You Can't Kill the Spirit* (November 2018), which contains around 150 images – photographs, leaflets, newspaper cuttings, diaries – from the archives kept by Houghton Main WAPC Pit Camp. The other, *The Vigil*, written at the time but only completed and published 25 years later, tells a detailed story of the Vane Tempest Pit Camp in County Durham. Maxine Peake's 2018 theatre production of her radio play *Queens of the Coal Age* is about the occupation of Parkside Colliery by WAPC during the 1992-93 campaign. Following the 1992-93 campaign a drama documentary called *Nice Girls*, which the women from Trentham pit camp were involved in making with Peter Cheesman, played at the Vic in Stoke in 1993 and 1994, and in Paris 1995. An audio visual recording of this is available at the National Theatre archive. And in 1996, the Trentham women produced a film, *We are not defeated*.

The background and context to the 1992-93 fight against pit closures

One hundred and twenty five collieries had closed between the end of the miners' strike in 1985 and 1992. The 1992 announcement of a further 31 pit closures by John Major's Tory government aimed to finish the job started in 1984. The closures were to prepare a scaled-down coal industry for privatisation. By the end of 1994 no collieries remained in public ownership, and in 2015 Kellingley, the last deep mine, was closed. Research from the TUC shows the long-term impact we see today of the loss of secure jobs and the decline in the strength of trade unions to campaign and protect workers' rights – from 13.2 million unionised workers in 1979, to 6.2 million in 2015-16.[1] One in ten UK workers are in precarious jobs, including those in the gig economy, with less access to sick pay, redundancy and job protection, while zero-hours contract workers earn a third less than average employees.

The announcement that 10 of the 31 pits earmarked for closure would do so with immediate effect was the impetus for the women's pit camps. In December 1992, National Women Against Pit Closures called for the setting up of WAPC pit camps at as many of these ten pits as possible. The fire, spirit and determination of women from 1984–85, from Greenham Common and other struggles where women had played a central role, were rekindled. In January 1993, seven pit camps were set up – at Grimethorpe, Houghton Main and Markham Main in South Yorkshire, Parkside in Lancashire, Rufford in Nottinghamshire, Trentham Colliery in Stoke, and Vane Tempest in the Durham coalfield. Many of the pit camps carried on night and day, seven days a week throughout the cold winter from January 1993 for five months or longer, fighting until the end.

The images and the story outlined in *You Can't Kill the Spirit* were replicated in all the pit camps. '*One of the first things we did was set up the brazier, which was kept burning throughout the struggle. It represented what we were fighting for – the spirit of resistance and solidarity of the mining communities.'* It was also the focal point for everyone to gather – the women from the camp, miners coming to sign on for work at the pit, local people, visitors and supporters. It was somewhere to keep warm, to support each other, share a cuppa, to talk about what next in the campaign, to share ideas, stories, music and our lives…. and to make sure we were there for however long it took to win.

At Houghton Main Pit Camp the practical challenges, as well as ideas for campaigning, became a focus for weekly meetings. Common to all the pit camps, the time of the year and the weather meant shelter was a priority. For all the camps the support was heartening with individuals and local councils donating caravans and portacabins and people bringing food and donations to help keep the campaign going. *'We set up headquarters in the portacabin, where we*

Around the brazier

had the visitors' book, information and, of course, the kettle. Two caravans became our home from home for the duration of the struggle,' with at least two women staying overnight each and every night – sometimes children as well. They loved it... camping in the pit yard! *'We wanted to organise in a way that would mean we could keep going for as long as it took. We had learnt that from the strike – we had held out for a year before; we could do it again, if necessary.'*

Ways of organising

Women have often had to organise in a different way from men; we have had to because of our traditional and pivotal role in family life. Experiences in 1984–85, and changing expectations as a result, as well as the campaigns of the women's liberation movement over many decades, meant there were some changes in the roles of men and women. However, women usually still took the main responsibility for children and the home. Women have had to be adept at weaving the threads of life together to make sure there are no loose ends. We have had to ensure there are meals on the table, care for our children and (for some) our parents or other relatives, and go to work if we had a paid job. We had to find ways of juggling our other responsibilities with running the pit camp and organising the campaign – locally and nationally – but we knew we could do it; we were women, we were strong!

There were key aspects and themes to the way the women's pit camps were organised and operated that we hope will provide inspiration for future struggles, and we were drawing on the spirit shown by women from the past, in particular the working class women from mining communities in 1984-85 and the women from Greenham Common, who camped out for many years to campaign against American cruise missiles based at Greenham Common in Berkshire. These themes – involving the local and the wider community; sharing skills, information and resources; involving our children and our families; being creative and having fun – meant we were involving as many women as possible and ensured we were able to keep going, building support week by week, in for the long haul, determined to win.

We also made links and supported other struggles – for example, visiting the picket lines at Burnsalls, Smethick, where Asian women were on strike, Middlebrook Mushroom, Timex and other struggles led by women. We organised Women in Struggle meetings, bringing together women from different struggles to build solidarity between us all. Fran visited Houghton and Grimethorpe pit camps with solidarity greetings from the NUT. *'It was always a great experience to meet with the women fighting to stop pit closures...their solidarity, determination and courage was humbling and a brilliant example of how working class people can unite to fight back. We need some of that spirit today.'*

Twenty-five years later, it is easy to forget that we did not have the same 'organising tools' we have now – no Facebook, WhatsApp or Instagram; very little, if any, use of email or digital photography. We organised using 'snail mail' and telephone trees. There were several 'trees' or 'branches' so we could get messages out quickly. The camp diary and message book were crucial for keeping each other informed – especially vital things like how to make sure we kept our access to the pit toilet!

We wanted to organise in a way that involved lots of women; we needed to cover the rota twenty-four hours a day, seven days a week, month after month, as well as taking part in the wider campaign – talking at meetings, going on demonstrations, raising funds for the campaign and producing publicity material. It was challenging. We wanted everyone to feel included, safe and respected. We wanted the children, as well as other family members and friends, to be involved, so they would understand what we were doing and why.

Creating and sustaining

Ensuring we could keep the pit camp going month after month, as well as going out campaigning and organising, was difficult. We needed to be very creative and imaginative, to motivate everyone to stay involved, and to encourage more women to join us. It was important to keep up the morale of the miners who continued to sign up for work every shift, and to raise the profile of the campaign: 'Not 31, not 21, not 10, No Pit Closures'. As David, a Houghton miner and father of three young children explained, *'The women's pit camp kept spirits going for the lads – we knew we weren't on our own – we weren't isolated. It definitely made a difference.'*

We shared ideas and were creative throughout our campaign. We made a banner together, made T-shirts and badges, made music and sang, produced leaflets and posters, always trying to come up with ideas to raise the profile. We held carnivals and events in the pit yard, shared stories, designed a commemorative plate to raise funds for the campaign – activities common to many of the other pit camps.

We made the banner at the local youth centre at the top of the pit lane soon after setting up the pit camp. It was a collective effort. The image of the banner was projected onto the material, and everyone had a go painting it (a bit like painting by numbers!), and the children were involved in making their own T-shirts, badges and banners. Many of the children still remember being involved – it has shaped their politics.

'At the pit camp and demonstrations I always felt part of something important .... something huge so it was hard to understand how we couldn't win. .... the pit camps were part

of history – a part that I was participating in.' Tom (aged 10 in 1993)

Campaigning and demonstrating

With National Women Against Pit Closures and the other pit camps, we were actively involved in helping to organise the national WAPC demonstration in London on Saturday 6 February 1993, as well as local marches and other joint meetings and events. The national WAPC demonstration was huge. Later in February 1993 we found out that Michael Heseltine was visiting South Yorkshire at the end of the month to open a new foundry in Balby near Doncaster. We decided to give him a Yorkshire miners' greeting, and with the activists in Doncaster we organised a picket. Some children still remember with amusement the rhyming slogan we put on our banner: *'He's a git, he's a swine, what's his name? ....!'*

Under pressure from the campaign and public opinion in the autumn of 1992, the Department for Trade and Industry had agreed a coal review. It presented the report in March 1993. It stated that *'the government recognised that in the difficult wider economic context the speed and scale of the closures announced by British Coal in October 1992 were too great to be acceptable to a wide body of public and parliamentary opinion'.* However, there was no intention to reprieve the ten most threatened pits, despite the report recognising *'the pain and hardship this would cause both to individuals and to communities'.*

On 5 March 1993, the NUM, NACODS and the RMT all balloted their members, asking them to vote in favour of a 24-hour stoppage as part of a rolling programme of industrial action to stop plans to close the 31 pits.[2] At Houghton Main, as in other pit camps, we organised around the ballot, to build public and community support and to support the miners at Houghton Main pit to vote 'yes'. This was the focus of our hot air balloon event and carnival in the pit yard on 4 March 1993, the eve of the ballot, when the balloon took off from the pit yard, travelling miles over the South Yorkshire coalfields, with three women from the camp, trailing the banner, 'Not 31, not 21, not 10, NO PIT CLOSURES'. It returned later to give the children, and some of the adults, a short ride up above the pit yard.

The balloon flies across the coalfields of South Yorkshire

A demonstration was organised in Houghton for 27 March with the local NUM branch, around the local village, with the children holding the placards of all the 125 pits closed since 1985. We were encouraging and building solidarity for people to support the call for one-day strikes on 2 and 16 April 1993.

But, despite all the public support for keeping the pits open, British Coal moved to close the ten pits, including Houghton Main, Grimethorpe and Markham Main as quickly as possible. This was done without adopting any long-term approach to the reduction of dependency on coal, or developing long-term, sustainable support for coal mining communities.

Our demonstration in Houghton was followed by two days of national strike action. Having won the ballot for strike action on 5 March, the two 24-hour strikes on 2 and 16 April saw over six million people staying away from work. On 23 April the pit camp had its 100 days' birthday. On 29 April, in frustration at the way things were going, and to raise the profile of the campaign, together with the other South Yorkshire pit camps, we organised an occupation of the National Coal Board office.

We wanted to highlight the awful injustice of closing the ten pits, despite the High Court ruling in December 1992 that the government had failed to fully consult with the unions and that the immediate closure was illegal. A later High Court ruled at the end of May that there had been sufficient consultation and it was lawful for British Coal to close the pits. In fact, they had effectively already done so by the end of April, by bribing the miners with enhanced redundancy, with only days to accept or lose the offer.

Blackmail

The Women Against Pit Closures press release, 29 April, from the Women's Pit Camps in South Yorkshire stated: '*To*

Children lead the march through Houghton

express our anger against British Coal and the Government's latest dirty tricks towards the miners by blackmailing them into closing their own pits, women from the pit camps have organised this sit-in at British Coal Headquarters, to bring to people's attention the outrage that is felt in the mining communities of the pits affected by the closures. British Coal are bribing the men in a very underhand way into accepting higher redundancy pay to close the pits straight away, before any review procedure has been completed, an offer which at this present time the miners have difficulty in refusing. This is British Coal shutting pits through the back door.'

On 4 May 1993 the NUM wrote formally to us at the pit camp, confirming that the pit had closed. The Branch Secretary wrote *'on behalf of the branch, to give our sincere thanks... without your support the fight would have been lost months ago... We hope links with yourselves can continue as we now try to make a future for ourselves.'*

Occupy!

WAPC had organised an occupation of the office buildings at Markham Main early on in the campaign, in December 1992, raising the profile of the campaign and leading the way to the setting up of Markham Main Pit Camp the following month. Further occupations took place the following year, including women from Trentham Pit Camp who occupied the headgear at Trentham Colliery, and during the Easter weekend 1993, women from Grimethorpe and Parkside occupied Parkside colliery, the story relived in Maxine Peake's play.

Thinking about it 25 years on, Elaine from Grimethorpe Pit Camp said: '*At least we went down fighting. And that matters. That matters.*' Anne shared the same sentiments: '*Well at least I did something to try and prevent this*'... '*I work with the homeless now... there's some of them lads – they're mainly 18 to 26 – their parents probably never had a job, they're never going to have a job, there's no job round here... them kids – what chance have they got?*' Dot from Thurnscoe & Houghton Main Pit Camp: '*There's nothing permanent for them at all... our grandson didn't know if he were working next day, he had to wait 'til they phoned him... this is what makes me angry when they talk about more people in work.*'

Spirit of Solidarity: *You Can't Kill the Spirit!*

On 22 May 1993 we held a big Women in Struggle meeting and our *You Can't Kill the Spirit* party to thank everyone for all their support. Our last act in the pit yard was to spray-paint the car park: we wanted to show that no-one could kill our spirit. As we accepted that the struggle to save Houghton Main and the other pits had been lost, like the other pit camps, we ended on a positive note with the end-of-camp party. Even if we had lost this struggle, we wanted to carry on acting in solidarity with other people challenging injustices.

The aftermath of the closure of the pits was as predicted. The huge cost of closing the pits and the impact on mining communities had been well documented. *The Government Review* of March 1993 recognised the impact of the closures and the devastating blow they would inflict on the mining communities, though little was done to soften this blow.

What happened in the 1980s and the aftermath of the attack on the steel and mining industries was still at the forefront of people's minds in 1992–93. We knew that no thought had been given to the consequences of closing the pits on the lives of individuals, families and communities: the mass unemployment, closure of small businesses in communities and the loss of hope created by multi-generational unemployment. The consequences are still being felt today, 25 years later. But many of us remain active in different campaigns now – we learnt a lot – and that spirit of solidarity endures.

'You can't obliterate from the human spirit two things –
The flame of anger at injustice and
The flame of hope for a better world.'
Tony Benn, May Day rally in Chesterfield in 1993

NOTES

(1) 'Outsourcing public services is damaging for staff and service users, says TUC', TUC Report, 3 March, 2015; 'How union membership has grown – and shrunk', *The Guardian*, 30 April, 2010.

(2) NUM, NACODS and the RMT: The National Union of Mineworkers, The National Association of Colliery Overmen, Deputies and Shotfirers and the Rail, Maritime and Transport Workers Union balloted their workers to take strike action to support the miners' struggle.

Copies of our book, *You Can't Kill the Spirit* (ISBN 9781999702625) are available by emailing: SWAPCPitCamp1993@gmail.com

Copies of *The Vigil* are available from jean.spence@btinternet.com

Our final act... spray painting the pit yard

Coal's last rites

On 13 October 1992 Tory Minister Michael Heseltine proposed the closure of 31 out of the then still working 50 deep coal mines in the UK. A massive wave of protest followed, together with several very large demonstrations.

A year later the last rites of the coal industry were administered. In a meeting at the Department of Trade and Industry (DTI), Energy Minister Tim Eggar told the mining unions that he would not order a moratorium on pit closures. Nor was he interested in a dialogue, unless it was to discuss privatisation.

Paul Routledge commented in *The Independent* (17/10/1993), 'Perhaps only a minister with Mr Eggar's legendary thick skin could have scheduled a meeting on the future of the coal industry on the first anniversary of his chief's announcement of the closure of more than half the nation's collieries.'

So what happened? A year before, 250,000 people went on the streets of London to protest about the government's plans to allow 30,000 miners to be sacked in a billion-pound redundancy operation. Middle England rose in revolt, and 3,000 marchers in Cheltenham carried placards demanding 'Sack John Major, Not The Miners'. Women Against Pit Closures set up camps protesting against the proposed closures outside seven pits.

These protests forced a Cabinet rethink, and led to Michael Heseltine's March 1993 White Paper *The Prospects for Coal* which 'saved' 21 of the original hit-list with the promise of £500m in subsidies - if the industry could find new markets for cheap coal. But by October 1993 nine of those reprieved collieries had closed, with a further 10 over the following months. The White Paper was a ploy that worked successfully to get Heseltine off the hook. Not a penny of the subsidy money was spent.

It was a cynical exercise by Major's government, who seemed oblivious to the destructive impact of these closures on the mining communities affected. The market was rigged against coal. The two privatised electricity generating companies, Powergen and National Power, didn't want coal, and DTI approval for the 'dash for gas' accelerated, with gas rapidly displacing coal.

What followed was, in Cecil Parkinson's words, the 'ultimate privatisation' with the coal industry broken up into five packages and sold to the highest bidder.

Richard Budge's RJB Mining successfully bid for three of the five parts of British Coal offered for sale by the government – the complete English industry, which comprised 17 pits plus land and opencast interests. In 2001 Budge was sacked as chief executive of RJB Mining and the company was renamed UK Coal. Its last deep mine, Kellingley in North Yorkshire, closed in December 2015.

Contributors

Huw Beynon is Emeritus Professor of the Wales Institute of Social and Economic Research, Data and Methods (WISERD) at Cardiff University. He edited *Digging Deeper: Issues in the Miners' Strike,* Verso 1985, and has researched and written widely on the impact of pit closures upon miners, their wives, partners and children and upon coal mining communities.

Flis Callow, Marilyn Haddington, Debbie Matthews and Caroline Poland were active participants in the Houghton Main Women's Pit Camp. Their book *You Can't Kill the Spirit* vividly describes 'the untold story of the women who set up camp to stop pit closures'.

Tony Garnett has produced television dramas for the BBC Wednesday Play: *Up the Junction* (1965), *Cathy Come Home* (1966); films: *Kes* (1969) and *Family Life* (1971), and TV series: *Between The Lines* (1992) and *This Life* (1996). His memoir *The Day The Music Died* was published in 2016.

Ray Goodspeed was a founder member of Lesbians and Gays Support the Miners in 1984 and also took part when it reformed in 2014. He is an officer of his local Constituency Labour Party. He has also been involved in many campaigns that seek to bring together the LGBT community with labour movement, socialist, internationalist and trade union causes.

Nicholas Jones reported the 1984-85 strike for BBC Radio. He was a BBC Industrial and Political Correspondent with the BBC from 1972-2002. His reflections on the pit dispute and commentaries on Mrs Thatcher's cabinet papers relating to the strike can be accessed at *www.nicholasjones.org.uk*

Pete Lazenby joined the *Wharfedale Observer* in Otley in 1967 as a trainee reporter. He joined the *Yorkshire Evening Post* in 1972 and became Industrial Correspondent in 1974. He now works for the *Morning Star.*

Morag Livingstone is an experienced short film maker, writer and documentary photographer. Her feature-length documentary *Belonging: The Truth Behind The Headlines* achieved nine film festival recognition awards including three winners for 'Best Documentary'.

Julian Petley was one of the authors of *Media Hits the Pits* (1985). He is Professor of Film and Television at Brunel University, and a former chair of the Campaign for Press and Broadcasting Freedom.

Jean Spence and **Carol Stephenson.** Jean was active in the Vane Tempest Vigil, Seaham 1993 and edited *The Vigil (1993).* Carol and Jean have published articles about gender, community and political activism with reference to coal mining, particularly in County Durham.

Granville Williams is the coordinator for CPBF(North). He edited the first edition of *Shafted* and has also edited *Settling Scores: The Media, the Police and the Miners' Strike in 2014; Pit Props: Music and International Solidarity in the 1984-85 Miners' Strike* (2016), and *The Flame Still Burns: The Creative Power of Coal* (2017).